Keys to the Qur'an

Keys to the Qur'an

Volume 3
Commentary on Surah Yasin

Zahra Publications

First published in 1993
Distributed & Re-published in 2018
Publisher: Zahra Publications
www.sfhfoundation.com
www.zahrapublications.com

Designed and typeset in South Africa by Quintessence Publishing
Cover Design by Mizpah Marketing Concepts
Project Management by Quintessence Publishing

Set in 11 point on 13 point, Garamond
Printed and bound by Lightning Source

ISBN (Printed Version) – Paperback: 978-1-928329-02-2

TABLE OF CONTENTS

PUBLISHER'S NOTE

This series began in 1981 as part of the teachings of the Holy Qur'an in the United States and Europe. The 5 volumes were first printed as Beams of Illumination from the Divine Revelation under the Zahra Publications imprimatur. It was printed as a set of 5 volumes under the title Keys to the Qur'an by Garnet Publishing. The present publication combines the previous 5 volumes in 5 parts under one cover, published by Zahra Publications.

Numerous people had helped and worked to realize the original editions of these commentaries including Muna H. Bilgrami, Aliya Haeri, Batool Ispahany, Kays Abdul Karim Mohammed, Dr. Salah al-Habib, Luqman Ali, Hasan Jobanputra, Christopher Flint and Syed Muyhi al-Khateeb, Dr. Yaqub Zaki and Dr. Omar Hamza. The current publication was assisted by Farhad Motara, Yunus Ismail and Leyya Kalla.

ABOUT THE AUTHOR

Shaykh Fadhlalla Haeri is a spiritual philosopher and writer whose role as a teacher grew naturally out of his own quest for self-fulfillment. Since childhood he has been attracted to scientific investigation and intellectual pursuit. He was born in Karbala, Iraq, and is a descendant of several generations of well-known and revered spiritual leaders.

After a stint in industry and consulting, he embarked on teaching, writing and meditating.

His awareness of global realpolitik compelled him to seek a truth that would reconcile the past with the present, the East and West. His discovery affirms that One Cosmic Reality is the source behind all known and unknown states.

Shaykh Haeri's unifying perspective emphasizes practical, actionable knowledge of self-transformation. It provides a natural bridge between different approaches to spirituality,

offering common ground of higher knowledge for various religions, sects and secular outlooks.

His main work has been to make traditional Islamic teachings more comprehensible and widely available to the modern seeker through courses and publications. Shaykh Fadhlalla Haeri is currently engaged in lecturing and writing books and commentaries on the Holy Qur'an and related subjects, with particular emphasis on ethics, self-development and gnosis ('irfan').

With a lifetime's experience of contemplation, research, and insights, he shares what it means to live in the light of the Absolute in a relative world and maintains that spiritual awakening is potentially available to all.

INTRODUCTION

The Qur'an was revealed in an instant, issuing forth from a realm beyond time. Its unfolding within the domain of time, however, occurred over a span of twenty-three years, for it was necessary for the message to be fully absorbed, integrated and applied existentially. The message was, and continues to be, that Allah is the Reality behind all that one witnesses. He is beyond description and beyond perception by the senses. He has Attributes, but nothing can be associated with Him. He can only be alluded to. We are therefore taught to talk about Allah only in terms of His Attributes, not of His Essence.

The Qur'an came as a complete revelation, as one unit in space, as one instant in time, like a bolt of lightning that hits the sleeper and stuns him into wakefulness. It descended as a stream of truth upon the heart of the Prophet Muhammad, peace and blessings be upon him, his family and his righteous Companions;[1] for the Muhammadan application of the truth of the Qur'an is the vital complement. To try to understand the Qur'an without the Prophet would have been comparable to an attempt to use a medical manual with no previous medical experience: the manual is of little use to one who has no training. To know the meaning of reality one must follow a particular path of application. Thus, Islam is based on both the Qur'an and the Prophetic way (*Sunnah*).

All the basic principles of knowledge are contained in this book. It is an existential guide for perpetual life. The message of the Qur'an is based on balance, on living a life which inevitably leads to a better future, materially and morally, both

---

1   It is customary, whenever the name of the Prophet Muhammad is mentioned, to invoke the peace and blessings of Allah upon him, his family and his righteous Companions.

on an individual and a social level.

The purpose of the Qur'an is for its message to be absorbed by the hearts of men. If there is no impact, then the remedy is only palliative. Superficial use of the Qur'an may be likened to a person who, hearing that vitamins are useful for the body's health, takes some indiscriminately. The vitamins are likely to be of some benefit, but they would have been far more useful had he known his specific condition and the properties of the vitamins, how they interact and enhance each other as well as how they might occasionally counteract one another. With this knowledge he would have been able to benefit maximally by taking the correct type and dosage. We hope to approach and use the Qur'an in this way.

The ability to derive meaning and knowledge from the Qur'an depends upon having the correct approach, and a humble, pure intention to attain knowledge. The assumption that one already knows something can be a hindrance. Therefore, one must be bereft, recognizing one's poverty, ignorance, weakness and need for knowledge and transformation. To approach the Qur'an, the seeker must possess the right courtesy (*adab*) which will serve as a key to awaken the knowledge of the Qur'an already contained within the heart.

Drawing from the Qur'an, penetrating into it, integrating it into one's life and thus learning from it, require both outer and inner courtesy (*adab*). If we approach the Qur'an with courtesy and love, it will unfold to us its values.

To gain the blessings and mercy of Reality through this ultimate, complete and balanced book of wisdom, one must appreciate its historical context and the overall environmental and ecological situation at the time of its descent. This includes understanding the civilization and culture of the time and place of its revelation, and more specifically, the nature of the people and their nomadic values. The Arab nomads of the Prophet's time, like nomads in general, were highly sensitized to their environment, for they had little protection from it. Because of the extreme harshness of their environment, the Bedouin Arabs lived continually on the verge of moral danger; they had therefore developed extremely alert, agile and intuitive minds which were highly attuned to everything around them. Furthermore, the nomadic system of the Bedouin people was in constant conflict with the civic system of the city dwellers. Whenever the nomadic and sedentary cultures met, conflict as well as renewal occurred.

The qualities most highly valued in nomadic cultures were nobility, courage and generosity. The people of the desert were self-reliant and fiercely independent. They would not bow to another human being. The leader emerged naturally, and was recognized because of his qualities and character. In this system it was likely that the next leader would come from the present leader's clan or be related to him. In nomadic culture, the home, or tent, of the tribal chief was always open, and yet it was customary for people not to go begging, so as not to demean themselves. Thus, generosity was naturally balanced with integrity, self-esteem and patience.

The Qur'an arose amidst the Arab culture and a simpler way of life than ours, but its universal message enlivened the hearts of diverse people, even during the Prophet's lifetime. It is helpful if we are aware of the environment in Mecca and Medina at the time of the Qur'anic revelation in order then to apply it to the social and cultural situation of our time, for the Qur'an is a guide book in an actual prescriptive sense.

The Muhammadan path, as it evolved over the course of time, is inextricably linked, step by step, to the revelation of the Qur'an. It began with the acknowledgement of the Oneness of God and it ended with the establishment of a very strong community in which individuals, having completely recognized the laws governing human relationships, interacted in a manner that allowed each one to develop spiritually to his or her full capacity. The righteous Companions followed their

Prophet Muhammad and thereby became established in their knowledge of God.

The Prophet saw in everyone the highest possible potential to be awakened to the higher inner knowledges. He recognized in all situations, even those which appeared to other men as afflictive, nothing other than Allah's mercy and compassion. He had the ability to see the ignorance that veils the hearts of men and causes them to act incorrectly, and he acted with understanding towards them. He worked to purify men's hearts, to help them evolve towards awakening to the inner life.

The few Muslims who were with the Prophet in the beginning were constantly subjected to oppression and opposition. The Prophet, wanting to save his small group of original followers, recommended that many travel to a place of safety, since living in Mecca had become impossible; for as their numbers grew so did opposition to them. The atmosphere had become increasingly polarized and hostile. The Muhammadan light, translated into a code of conduct, had become a major threat to the tribal habits of a people who took fierce pride in their ancestral ways. Their factional loyalties often led them to resort to brute force, with total disregard for logic, reason and human values. This polarization in Mecca would lead inevitably to violence.

In contrast to the clans in Mecca, some of the people of Medina saw light and usefulness in the message of Islam. Whereas the people of Mecca regarded the Prophet as no more than the son of one of their own kind, and could not accept his prophethood, the people of Medina, an agrarian people who were settled and more receptive, welcomed the Prophet and his followers, who upon arrival immediately began to build a mosque and homes: they embarked upon creating a community. But with a community also came problems: 'Surely We have created man in affliction' (90:4).

VOLUME 3: DESCRIPTION

Surat Yā Sīn is the heart of the Qur'an (*qalb al-Qur'an*). It is the chapter (*surah*) of the Qur'an which is read over the dead; therefore it is a chapter of great importance to the living. Should one seek to know the meaning of life, one must experience death, for man has come from the non-physical realm and he is swiftly proceeding towards it again. Knowledge is based on opposites. Man's apprehension of knowledge depends upon the condition of his heart. If the condition of his heart is pure and receptive, he sees perfection in every aspect of every situation he finds himself in. The Qur'an allows one to fathom the unfathomable.

CHAPTER 36
Surat Yā Sīn: Introduction

The prevailing disease of our present age is denial of the One Reality that underlies, permeates, encompasses and yet stands apart from existence. To awaken the heart of the seeker to this Reality, the teacher attempts to tap the remedy drawn from the unity and timelessness of the Truth, the source of which is within that very heart. The source book of Truth, the all-encompassing Book of Reality, the key to unlocking the heart of the seeker on the path to divine knowledge, is the Qur'an. The absolute Truth is reflected in the Book, is further reflected through the purified heart of the believer (*mu'min*) and reaches out to illuminate every atom in creation.

For the proper approach to the Qur'an there must be the right intention and the right outer courtesy: the ritual ablution (*wudū*), the right courtesy in holding, opening and closing the Book, and even in where it is placed afterwards. Since it is the Book of Books, the correct approach is the vital key that allows us to profit best from its reading and recitation.

The traditionally classical approach to the Qur'an is to study it from the standpoint of linguistics, history (the specific occasions of the revelation of certain verses) and other relevant aspects. Having done that, should one seek greater insight, should one want to dive more deeply into this ocean, one must be completely empty of any notions, expectations or reactions. To obtain the greatest inward benefit the reader must be completely void. One must be totally and utterly in a state of purity. This means that the Qur'an is approached with the maximum fearful awareness (*taqwā*) and with the utmost openness from a pure heart that is open in the sense that anything may come to it or nothing at all, depending upon the extent of one's receptivity. If the approach be impure, contact with the Qur'an will be superficial. Nevertheless, this will still be a positive and beneficial experience for whosoever approaches the Qur'an with the slightest outer propriety so long as he is not doing so just to criticize or analyze it.

The true inner courtesy owed to the Qur'an is that one should be as though in the presence of the King of kings, in the presence of the Ultimate, Whose words have been sung through the heart and by the tongue of His beloved Prophet Muhammad, peace and blessings be upon him, his family and his righteous Companions.[2] One should bring to life the realization that this divine song has come to one as a rare and precious gift; otherwise, its secrets will remain locked and inaccessible. For those who have the purest intentions the Qur'an is vast and its gifts are endless. Every time a seeker, scholar or commentator reflects on it as he progresses in his life, with an ever deeper experience of the purest mode of approach he finds a fresh spring.

Our interest is both the outward (*ẓāhirī*) as well as the inward (*bāṭinī*) approach to the Qur'an, because we are interested in unity (*tawḥīd*). Islam is the most perfect way of life and path to knowledge because it is the journey of unity. If it is original Islam, it will take one to the knowledge of unity, from faith (*īmān*) to absolute certainty (*yaqīn*). 'Alī ibn Abī Ṭālib said: 'If every unknown thing were made known to me, I would not increase in certainty.' One should reflect upon the state of inner knowledge that 'Alī speaks about, that absolute certainty about the knowledge of Reality.

---

2   It is customary, whenever the name of the Prophet Muhammad is mentioned, to invoke the peace and blessings of Allah upon him, his family and his righteous companions.

The whole concern is about the full knowledge of unity, not about information. All the verses of the Qur'an must be of benefit right now. Every aspect of the Qur'an is to be taken and used by those who are desperate for the knowledge of Reality, those who aspire to know Allah. We are not only interested in the Qur'an as a historical document. Nothing ever finishes or changes. What was in man's heart millennia ago still exists in man's heart today. All the elements are the same: trust-mistrust, love-hate, peace-violence, compassion-anger, comfort-discomfort, illness-health, life-death. The self (*nafs*) is one consciousness and contains the full spectrum of these human characteristics within it, high and low. In every heart they exist in different proportions, while varying circumstances draw on one characteristic more than another, whether it be the heart of an ordinary man or of a prophet. The difference is that a characteristic such as anger in a prophet is directed against injustice and ignorance in man, whereas the anger of an ordinary man may be reactionary, emotional or unjust, because he is capable of making mistakes. A true man of Allah, and certainly a prophet or messenger of Allah, may exhibit all the lower characteristics of the ego but operate in a direction that is positive and conducive to man's ultimate awakening. A prophet hates: he hates ignorance and the self-imposed blindness of men. He hates injustice and man's unwillingness to move, hanging on to the past, to some illusion he inherited from his forefathers or that was conditioned by his own previous experiences.

The watchful traveler on this short journey recognizes these lower aspects of the ego in himself through his true submission and perpetual vigilance. He has a yearning (*himmah*) for knowledge that drives him on and on in his striving against unbelief (*jihād*), against these negative elements in himself. The battle is both outward and inward, for: 'He is the Outwardly Manifest and the Inwardly Hidden, and He is the First and the Last.' We notice today that the collapse of the so-called Muslim world is the natural outcome of Muslims' having neglected to take on fully the path to unitary knowledge. People talk about Islam and even teach Islam, but this cannot be the same as any other type of teaching for this teaching must be embodied, otherwise it is worse than useless.

Sūrat Yā Sīn is the heart of the Qur'an (*qalb al-Qur'ān*). It is the chapter (*sūrah*) of the Qur'an which is read over the dead; therefore it is a chapter of great importance to the living. Should one seek to know the meaning of life, one must experience death, for man has come from the non-physical realm and he is swiftly proceeding towards it again. Knowledge is based on opposites. Man's apprehension of knowledge depends upon the condition of his heart. If the condition of his heart is pure and receptive, he sees perfection in every aspect of every situation he finds himself in. The Qur'an allows one to fathom the unfathomable.

Sūrat Yā Sīn is also about the Prophet Muhammad and it is addressed directly to the bearers of the unitary message who continue to carry out the message. Whoever takes on fully the message of unity is considered a representative (*khalīfah*) of Allah. He becomes a true slave (*'abd*) liberated from enslavement by the absence of himself and continues to exist — in the station of on-goingness — in his Lord.

CHAPTER 36

Surat Yā Sīn

بِسْمِ ٱللَّهِ ٱلرَّحْمَٰنِ ٱلرَّحِيمِ

In the Name of Allah, the Beneficent, the Merciful.

يسٓ ﴿١﴾

1. Yā Sīn

وَٱلْقُرْءَانِ ٱلْحَكِيمِ ﴿٢﴾

2. By the wise Qur'an,

Yā sīn is one of the names given to the Prophet Muhammad. It is also a shortened form of *Yā insān* which means 'O mankind!' or, 'O Human Being'. The *sūrah* (chapter) might also be addressed to the people of Antioch to whom the Prophet Jesus (*'Isā*) sent apostles. The term, the people of *Yā Sīn* signifies the Prophet's family (*Ahl al-Bayt*). This chapter begins by calling upon those among mankind who want to know, who want to follow the Prophet and connect directly with the prophetic message.

$$\text{إِنَّكَ لَمِنَ ٱلْمُرْسَلِينَ (٣)}$$

3. Surely you are one of the messengers,

This verse is addressed to the Prophet Muhammad. The message of the messengers is the message of unity (*tawhīd*). The source of the message is One, though the messengers sent from that source have been many, 'and you Muhammad are one of the messengers'. Since the Prophet Muhammad is the last of the messengers, he obviously encompasses all the previous messages. Regarding this the Qur'an says: 'We do not abrogate a sign or cause it to be forgotten without bringing one better than it or like it' (2: 106).

Even as normal, experiencing human beings, each time we have a new experience it should be better, subtler and more all-encompassing than the previous one. It is as though we are travelling in an evolutionary movement forward in time, but not in the Darwinian sense. We have not, biologically speaking, risen from the ape; rather, we have come from the lowest, the sperm cell, and have then developed into the most complex living organism. This is the inherent pattern of movement in the individual, as well as in the collective historical sense.

Historically, the Prophet Muhammad came from a line of earlier prophets who transmitted and practiced the message of Reality very simply. More than one tradition (*hadith*) tells us that there have been 124,000 prophets and messengers. Throughout different times and in many places numerous villages had a prophet in their midst. People were different then, purer and more transparent. The situations they lived in were generally more conducive to travelling the spiritual path.

The final message of the Qur'an encompasses, supersedes and abrogates all previous messages. It provides man with the complete model. Though the Prophet Muhammad rose from among the Arab peoples, he was the master and seal of all the messengers before him. Because he was the last, his message is universal, open to all and applicable by everyone wherever and whenever.

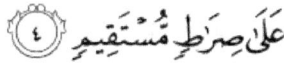

$$\textrm{عَلَىٰ صِرَٰطٍ مُّسْتَقِيمٍ}\ (٤)$$

4. On a straight path.

Still addressing the Prophet, Allah says: 'You are certainly on a clear path (*sirāt*), a straight and direct way.' The 'straight path' (*al – sirāt al-mustaqīm*) is the shortest distance between two points, between subject and object, between man and Allah. That is why it is direct, for it stretches from man to what he is always seeking, which is the All-Encompassing Reality. The understanding of unity (*tawhīd*) is the straight path (*al – sirāt al-mustaqīm*), but it cannot be the subject of mere intellectual study. One must move along the path of submission (*islām*), through belief (*īmān*) to sublime excellence (*ihsān*), until one begins to have glimpses of unity, through which one can then dive into the world of meaning.

If the goal of unity (*tawhīd*) is not constantly present in the minds of the Muslims, their Islam becomes diluted and falls by the wayside. Mosques become either totally empty or only superficially full, because most of the people there are attending only as a matter of form. In many parts of the Muslim world this is what one finds, because the path is no longer about remembrance of Allah (*dhikr Allah*), nor about wanting knowledge of Allah. In many places Islam itself has been put on a pedestal and is being worshipped instead of Allah. Islam, however, is a means to the knowledge of Allah, not the object itself.

We all love what is timeless. We all love what is absolute. Does anyone not want to live forever, past this life and on into the next? This means that we all love the One Who is forever living. The love of Allah, therefore, is already in our hearts, but we become diverted, we rationalize: 'Not now, tomorrow or next year, when I finish with this or that business.' We blame other people for our lack of time and all our other problems as well. The truth is that we only have ourselves to blame.

The knowledge of Allah is already written for us, either in this life or the next, so why not move for it now, while we can? We are going to be in that state later on, after tasting death, so why not try to discover what it means in this life, where it can be of use to us?

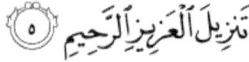

$$ \text{تَنزِيلَ ٱلْعَزِيزِ ٱلرَّحِيمِ} \ ⑤ $$

5. A revelation from the Mighty, the Merciful,

Since we are bound to the ground by the law of gravity, we naturally consider anything more exalted and divine to be 'higher', that is, it must transcend the natural barriers to which we are subject. Thus, the human view is that the message of Allah 'comes down' from on high, and this is reflected in the word translated as 'revelation', for *tanzīl* (literally means a descending. It is not that Allah is high or low: there is only Allah, and He — may He be exalted — inhabits no place. Man is earth-bound, food-bound, air-bound. The word for earth in Arabic is *ard*, which also means 'something one beats upon', because we are here to beat on the earth in the right manner in order to bring out what it contains, to take out our sustenance from it and thereby attain the right attitude of humility.

Since the word 'revelation' (*tanzīl*) is 'something that is sent down', it is divine and rare, for it is from the Mighty (*'Azīz*). It also, however, has mercy (*rahmah*) in it, so it is from Him Who bestows beneficence, *al-Rahman*. The Beneficent is His Attribute of All-Encompassing Mercy, universal mercy, the same for believer and non-believer, like the rain which falls upon everyone. The Beneficent covers everything, good and bad, because this is the decree of Allah. The Merciful, *al-Rahīm*, which is an intensive form of the word from the same root, is more specific, affecting particular individuals in a more intense but more limited way. Everything in existence is really under the decree of mercy of the Beneficent.

Take the poisonous snake for example. From man's point of view the creature is dreadful, a threat to life, yet it is contained within the all-encompassing domain of the Beneficent. If one is bitten by such a creature, this event is still within the domain of the Beneficent; but when one cries out 'Help!' to one's companion, the need for mercy is intensified and pin-pointed. The first aid administered for snake bite is, therefore, specific and is under the survey of the Merciful, *al-Rahīm*.

When we recognize the Beneficent at work behind every event in life, we know that the enemy or difficulty was really put there for our direct benefit. From this point of view the Attribute of beneficence is higher than mercy in as much as it encompasses everything. Thus, when both Divine Names are mentioned, the Beneficent is always mentioned before the Merciful. There is another way to understand the Attribute of mercy, that is, *al-Rahīm*. The form of this verbal noun implies an enduring quality. Thus it is distinguished from beneficence in that it applies to the believer, for Allah's mercy is not only intensified for the believer but endures into the next life as well.

$$\text{لِتُنذِرَ قَوْمًا مَّا أُنذِرَ ءَابَآؤُهُمْ فَهُمْ غَٰفِلُونَ ﴿٦﴾}$$

6. That you may warn a people whose fathers were not warned, so they are heedless.

The prophetic message is revealed in order to bring about fear of what is not conducive to the purification of the heart. The word for 'warn' here is the intensified verbal form of *nadhara* which basically means 'to make a vow'. Making a vow means taking decisive action by which one may ward off any non-conducive events. The word *qawm* in this verse, translated as 'a people', means any community or group of communities linked together by a single common denominator, such as language, worship or lifestyle.

The Arabs before Muhammad had not had a messenger from among themselves. There were many Christians and Jews living in their midst who were the 'People of the Book', but they had not had a messenger directly from their own people, from their own culture, to give them the news and the warning. People who are not warned are heedless, forgetful and in a state of distraction (*ghaflah*). The person who is heedless has his attention riveted somewhere less important than where it should be, as when, for example, while waiting for a train one is suddenly attracted by a poster display and consequently misses the train. One was attentive, but to something of no importance as compared to the original objective. The state of distraction the Qur'an speaks of is man's lack of attention towards Allah. He looks elsewhere instead, rather than single-mindedly concentrating on his Creator. Thus he becomes distracted by the creation and the creatures that inhabit it.

The people referred to in this verse heedlessly addressed themselves to the wrong direction, so were not receptive to the warning. Both the warning and the knowledge are inherent in man's own being, but their voice becomes smothered by acquired habits not in line with divine guidance. People become used to their habits and take comfort in them, for in their repetition is an aspect of perpetuity which is one of Allah's Attributes. Allah's Attributes permeate all substances and situations in creation. In the case of man, he must recognize that he has the choice of channeling the power of these Attributes towards what is conducive to his illumination or of channeling them into the illusion of the physical and material as the goal of existence.

Among man's worst enemies in life are his habits, even his good ones. The final stage of the seeker on the path of illumination and divine knowledge comes when he has to break all habits, even his expectation of direct knowledge. By the mercy of Allah, the right moment may come for him when the heart has retreated from the outer project for the final victory of abandonment. This stage is only for the person who is made ready by having no further expectations in this life. He is no longer expecting to 'see' Allah or 'meet' Allah — there is only Allah, so thinking that one is getting closer to Allah is a subtle form of association with Allah.

Breaking habits is necessary until one is in a state of perpetual awareness, accepting any situation as it comes, trusting that one will deal with it correctly, confident that Allah will guide one safely to its resolution. The one who has attained to this state, which is the state of witnessing (*shahādah*), will no longer spend an inordinate amount of time trying to out-guess and overcome any situation.

The purpose of the Qur'anic message, like the purpose of creation itself, is to enable man to travel from darkness into light. Physically the infant remains in the obscurity of the womb for nine months until it is forcefully expelled into the light. The habit of being in darkness is such that at birth it invariably cries. Similarly, man does not like change, because the never-changing is the basic substratum upon which all change in existence occurs. The people referred to in this verse were stubbornly holding on to the habits of their forefathers. The tribal and cultural habits in Arabia had remained stable and fixed for a very long time, if one can call the existence they had culture. There was amongst them much debauchery and little humanity. The miracle was that from amongst them came this immense light and peace, from the midst of that intense darkness, came the Perfect Man.

$$\text{لَقَدۡ حَقَّ ٱلۡقَوۡلُ عَلَىٰٓ أَكۡثَرِهِمۡ فَهُمۡ لَا يُؤۡمِنُونَ ۝}$$

7. Certainly the word has proven true for most of them, for they do not believe.

The truth is that Allah's decree affects all. They are in agony, the agony, affliction and turmoil of ignorance (*jāhiliyyah*). All man's troubles arise because of ignorance. Should a person become ill or be beset by an affliction and someone else explains how the affliction came about, then the person is somewhat relieved. Much of the trouble is reduced once one knows why it occurred in the first place. Knowledge brings certainty and security and therefore makes the heart tranquil.

Man's purpose is to dispel ignorance. Knowledge already exists within. Knowledge is from Allah's Attribute of *al-'Alim*, the Knower. This Attribute is never absent, so one's task is simply to strip away ignorance. Divine knowledge (*al-'ilm al-laduni*) is already with us, and to arrive at it we must learn prescriptive outer knowledge and proper courtesy, which are all based on the prophetic practices of the Prophet Muhammad.

The Prophet's outer practices of worship, such as prostration, proceeded from his original nature (*fitrah*). Following in his footsteps, we want to focus on the perfection of his original nature in order to gain knowledge; therefore we imitate his outer practices as completely as we can. The outer form is not the goal; the outer form is only important in order to obtain the inner, so that one may be reunified. Then while inwardly one has the life, light and love of the Prophet Muhammad, one outwardly follows his practice (*Sunnah*).

The people described in this verse lack faith and they will fail to find relief because of their distraction. Because of their own often inadvertent choice the people of heedlessness are veiled by their own habits; consequently, they are dulled and doomed. Faith and belief, however, provide a positive trust which enables one to realize that although one may be in ignorance now, eventually one will come to know that only the Beneficent and Merciful exists and that even though one is not completely satisfied and fulfilled at any particular moment, one will come to a point of scintillating freedom from all anxieties and afflictions experienced through ignorance. The path of belief leads to increased certainty.

إِنَّا جَعَلْنَا فِىٓ أَعْنَـٰقِهِمْ أَغْلَـٰلًا فَهِىَ إِلَى ٱلْأَذْقَانِ فَهُم مُّقْمَحُونَ ﴿٨﴾

8. Surely, we have placed chains on their necks reaching up to their chins, so they have their heads aloft.

The chains of ignorance are due to the lack of faith and submission, and their perpetual distraction causes such a lack. These chains are forged by one's subjective and selfish expectations, keeping one encased in rigidity, as if one's neck had been rendered immobile by them. Man cannot go through life without expectations but he can reorient the direction of his expectations in the way of Allah, in the way of discovering the nature of Reality, with no selfish attachment to the outcome.

The neck allows one to move the head and thus obtain a full range of vision. If the neck is encased up to the chin in a manacle, the ability to see is seriously hindered. Those devoid of faith and submission who are distracted by their inflexible conditioning are unable to obtain a clear view of Reality.

The nature and current of thought is the lock on the chain. Every thought has the characteristics of quality, direction and quantity. The rational person is constantly improving the quality of his thoughts as well as clarifying their direction, as a channel does to the flow of a river. If the amount of one's thoughts proves excessive they can flood uncontrollably and cause destruction.

The chains of expectations and attachments are forged as a person progresses through life. The more they are related to a person's egotistic habits and are designed to perpetuate comfort, the more we find such a person lacking in substance. Arrogance betrays extreme insecurity. When a person appears to be aggressively confident in himself, it means he is truly weak and uncertain. The possibility of his imminent downfall is too much to bear. The most basic Qur'anic analogy of this state is the arrogant assertion of the *Shaytān* (Satan), who exhibited his arrogance when he claimed that he was made of light. When Allah created Adam from clay and water, the *Shaytān* thought to himself, 'I am better than that', and this high opinion of himself precipitated his downfall.

The clearest manifestation of this phenomenon in human beings can be seen in tyrants. They appear to be so strong and in such complete control but suddenly they reach a point where they move from what appeared to be absolute control to no control at all, and the closer they move to their downfall the more arrogant they become. As they discover the frailty of the foundation upon which they have based their existence and the realization dawns that it is all about to slip away, the more they clutch at this false image of themselves, becoming ever more tyrannical. The true Muslim, on the other hand, is like a willow tree; he has deep roots of trust (*īmān*) and reliance (*tawakkul*) upon Allah, and so his outer aspect is as flexible as branches yielding to the wind. He is inwardly certain and outwardly flexible within a divinely inspired grid of correct conduct.

When the true Muslim must hide the nature of his beliefs because his life or property is in danger, he is not hiding from responsibilities, for this would be hypocrisy; rather, he is poised and ready. The moment the opportunity is right to defend against disbelief he does so, exerting himself to the utmost. Continued hindrance from being allowed to live and propagate Islam necessitates emigration (*hijrah*). There is no virtue in remaining in a place that is clearly headed for destruction. The Qur'an is specific about this. If one is living with people who are ultimately doomed because of their actions and yet one cannot help them, or at least combat them, then one must flee from them. Why should one form part of their final destruction? If a person negligently continues to stay, he deserves their doom as well.

Being stiff-necked is not the normal posture of the human being. A normal, healthy human being will have his head poised to go into prostration (*sajdah*), for he recognizes his total enslavement to Reality. As he is beloved of Allah his state of worship (*'ibādah*) outwardly expresses itself.

$$\text{وَجَعَلْنَا مِنْ بَيْنِ أَيْدِيهِمْ سَدًّا وَمِنْ خَلْفِهِمْ سَدًّا فَأَغْشَيْنَاهُمْ فَهُمْ لَا يُبْصِرُونَ ﴿٩﴾}$$

9. And We have placed a barrier in front of them and a barrier behind them, then We have covered them so they do not see.

Continuing the description of the people who are in fetters (*aghlāl*), following their old habits and not receptive to the message, Allah tells us that there is a barrier in front of them. The word for barrier, (*sadd*) comes from a verb meaning 'to block up', (*sadda*), as in reservoirs or dams. Here it signifies that they are not free in their actions, they are not spontaneous but dammed up and hemmed in. Thus their vision is shortsighted; they do not connect their present states with future ones nor their actions with their consequences. At any given moment, a human being is always the net product of his past actions and thoughts. If one is beset with troubles, illnesses or negative thoughts in the present, they are invariably the result of what one has done in the past. There is no escape in this world from the system of action and reaction.

'Then We have covered them so they do not see': as a result of their disconnectedness and, therefore, complete self-enslavement, a cover (*ghishāwah*) is placed over them. The implication is that they cannot see the laws governing a given situation, so they cannot comprehend what is happening to them. Where the light of knowledge does not shine the darkness of ignorance necessarily prevails: 'Allah is the Light of the heavens and the earth' (24:35).

The heavier the shackles of attachment, desire and expectation weigh, the more one is bound to the material world. If one is passionately attached to a car and one must take on loads, make promises and tell lies in order to hold on to it, one is completely shackled and enslaved. Arrogance naturally comes to our defense because there is no real foundation underlying our illusions. As one's arrogance increases, one is less able to connect actions and intentions from the present to the future, so one ends up blind and isolated. The moving stream is not seen. The hand of Allah behind all is not recognized.

The proof of blindness is visible: drudgery, anxiety, uncertainty and social unrest. The blind always blame everything on someone or something else; they fail to see that one gets exactly what one deserves, not what one desires.

The whole matter is about unity, and the further one moves along the path of unity the more one grows aware of the inter-connectedness of everything. The question of barriers is one only for those who do not act according to the moving stream of unity. This is why, for example, compartmentalized modern science is limited to such a great extent. Scientists who maintain a multi-disciplined approach are more successful since they perceive a continuum, but they also have to take account of the 'gaps' they see in the continuum, which make no sense to them. In reality there is no separation.

Whatever we do on the earth affects the entire cosmos, although it may not be measurable by our senses or sensory devices. Even the consumption of oxygen by the individual affects the total oxygen-carbon dioxide balance. The entire physical, mental and spiritual system of existence is completely interwoven, dependent. There is no separation in it. We cannot say, 'I end here. This is my house, my territory, I am an island unto myself.' If one's neighbor is poor and sick, it will affect one sooner or later in some way.

There is oneness of the world, and oneness of mankind. This awareness should always be present in our hearts. There is only Allah. 'He is the First, He is the Last, He is the Outwardly Manifest and He is the Inwardly Hidden.' With awareness and constant remembrance (*dhikr*) our attitudes become more purified and useful to us on this journey.

وَسَوَآءٌ عَلَيْهِمْ ءَأَنذَرْتَهُمْ أَمْ لَمْ تُنذِرْهُمْ لَا يُؤْمِنُونَ ﴿١٠﴾

**10. Alike it is to them whether you warn them or not,
they do not believe.**

It makes no difference whether or not one warns people who
are caught in this state, they will not come to trust in Allah
and realize that the purpose of existence is to know Him. So
stubborn and fixed are they in their rejection that they will
never accept that ignorance is only self-inflicted and that it
can only be overcome by submission, trust and by following a
divinely guided path which opens the door of knowledge.

If man's consciousness and vision are totally covered by
self-imposed limitations and narrow expectations, coloring
everything that comes to him, the clear message of warning
that he is at a loss and transgressing against himself will not get
through. The message that he is associating another with Allah
and thus concealing the truth will not touch his heart. Idols
can easily be eliminated, but the subtle idols of self-image, self-
opinion, insecurity, reputation, arrogance, position, vanity, love
of power, and so on, are more difficult to do away with.

When a person erects a barrier cutting off his innermost
dimension and the voice of the Messenger, then the signal will
not penetrate the consciousness in order to activate the seed
of faith (*īmān*). This seed is already implanted, but it must be
watered and nourished for it to burst open. People who are cut
off in this way will not come into faith whether or not they are
warned. No matter what one does, they will not wake up. But
the messenger continues to sing the song regardless, just as
the bird that is completely inspired must keep on singing. This
is the reason why even most Muslims are afraid of the true
men of Allah, not to speak of the messengers and prophets —
may Allah bless them all — for all those who fully imbibed the
knowledge of Truth have been totally single-minded in their
determination to deliver the message, whether it was heeded or

31

not, even under the threat of death.

The *āyah* (verse) tells the Prophet, and by extension all those who follow in his footsteps, to go and warn people without being disappointed. Disappointment will not affect one so long as one's appointment is by Allah. Warn in the way of Allah (*fī sabīl Allāh*) without being harsh or aggressive, in a good-hearted, good-natured way, without expecting any results whatsoever. It is all for one's own sake anyhow, for the reward is inherent in the action itself. The reward is freedom, because the action emanated from a state of submission and peace. Only when one rehabilitates oneself can one then begin to rehabilitate others.

إِنَّمَا تُنذِرُ مَنِ ٱتَّبَعَ ٱلذِّكْرَ وَخَشِيَ ٱلرَّحْمَٰنَ بِٱلْغَيْبِ فَبَشِّرْهُ بِمَغْفِرَةٍ وَأَجْرٍ كَرِيمٍ ۝

11. You only warn him who follows the reminder and fears the Beneficent in the Unseen, so give him the good news of forgiveness and a generous reward.

This is a specific injunction to the Prophet Muhammad, but it also applies to anyone calling people to Allah (*da'wah*). One can only warn those people who are following the reminder or remembrance (*dhikr*) of Allah. One can only warn those people who are likely to follow and take heed, remembering what is already within them of before time, before creation, consciously aware of the meaning and purpose of this creation, which is ingrained within them.

The people of remembrance are described elsewhere in the Qur'an as people who reflect upon creation. The meaning of the creation as it manifests outwardly is contained within the heart of man; by his reflection upon creation true remembrance takes place. Remembrance implies prior knowledge of something; when we say, 'I remember him', it means that we once knew that person and we are now recalling him. The knowledge of Allah is like that; it is already in our hearts, but we have just not remembered it.

The 'reminder' (*dhikr*) here specifically means the Qur'an, because it is the manifestation of remembrance. That remembrance is contained in all the revealed Books, the most comprehensive and unaltered of which is the Qur'an. The Qur'an reflects revealed truth so that one may uncover the primordial truth already imprinted within one's being. Then one must unify this revelation with action. One cannot just intellectualize: 'He must follow the reminder.' By this remembrance one begins to awaken, for single-minded remembrance brings about tranquility, which allows reflection.

Reflection in turn allows the genetic echo of the story of Reality to be heard. The scriptwriter's secret is already there. To arrive at its rediscovery one must enter the gate of submission and faith and move along the path of remembrance while unifying one's actions with one's intentions. "When one tries to remember the Truth within oneself, one stops remembering anything other than it. Put another way, whoever remembers his essential state of being is not addressing himself to any duality that we experience in this world. The message of the Qur'an cannot be separated from the Messenger through whom it comes, since the Messenger himself exemplifies the Book. The message and the Messenger show us the safe route to what is pure and pleasing to the Lord.

'And fears the Beneficent in the Unseen' means that one is fearful of transgression. *Khashyah* is a positive fear of doing something without intention and action being unified, or fearing that an ignorant action will result in one's downfall. *Khashyah* is fear of relapsing into remembering other-than-Allah and wariness lest actions should lead to the negative side of Allah's all-encompassing mercy (*rahmah*). The meaning of mercy can only be fully understood by experiencing affliction.

The *Shaytān*, the agent of affliction, can also be a friend. He is also slave of Allah, performing his clever and dreadful job by causing trouble, but that does not mean that one should befriend him. One must be ever vigilant, for one never knows when his horns will suddenly appear. The *Shaytān* does his job by keeping us moving, for the purpose of all affliction is abandoning the project of self-perpetuation in this world and thereby increasing the spiritual evolution of the self.

The perfect time and the perfect situation for making use of these afflictions is the present. What this verse is saying is that one can only get through to those who are constantly striving to be in a state of awareness, who have suffered enough, who know where and how they have transgressed and thus been afflicted so that they fear transgressing the bounds further and being cut off from Allah's pleasure. The Prophet Muhammad once said: 'What is permitted (*halāl*) is clear, and what is forbidden (*harām*) is clear. Between the two are many grey areas, so avoid them!' If one is uncertain about how to act, one should avoid taking any action as much as possible until one is certain.

The word 'Unseen' (*Ghayb*) be understood in two ways. First of all one does not yet clearly know what the boundaries surrounding Allah's pleasure are, but one accepts the truth of their existence. Secondly, it means the Realm of the Unseen (*'Ālam al-Ghayb*). Not only is there the physical realm perceived by our senses but there is also a realm of existence that is beyond perception by our sight. The two are connected.

'So give him the good news of forgiveness': after being given the positive warning, one is then given the good news. The word for 'good news' (*bushrā*) is etymologically related to three other words meaning 'to peel' (*bashara*), 'outer layer of skin' (*basharah*) and 'mankind' (*bashar*). We could say that the warning flays man's outer skin of apparent separation to reveal the connectedness, unity and perfection of creation.

From a subjective point of view we might fear inadvertently slipping out from under the umbrella of the Beneficent. The good news is that there is only the umbrella of the Beneficent; there is only a generous reward for that initial movement of trust and acceptance.

إِنَّا نَحْنُ نُحْيِ الْمَوْتَىٰ وَنَكْتُبُ مَا قَدَّمُوا وَءَاثَارَهُمْ وَكُلَّ شَىْءٍ أَحْصَيْنَاهُ فِىٓ إِمَامٍ مُّبِينٍ ﴿١٢﴾

12. Surely, We bring the dead to life, and We record what they have sent ahead, and the traces they have left behind. We have recorded everything in a clear Book.

This universe is based on the law of life and death in physicality as well as in meaning. Often people are inwardly dead. They may have the outward appearance of life but they are not enlivened. Elsewhere the Qur'an says: 'Follow Allah and the Prophet so that you may have life.' Though this verse is addressed to the living it implies that the full awakening of consciousness is the inner meaning of being brought to scintillating life. Once the self has been transformed the lower tendencies will wither away.

Allah says of those who have yielded themselves up to Him, those who have been slain in His way: 'And do not speak of those who are slain in Allah's way as dead. Rather, they are alive! But you do not perceive them' (2: 154).

The Prophet said in a famous tradition: 'Man is asleep; when he dies he wakes up.' He also said: 'Die before you die.' From this we may understand that death, whether physical or metaphorical, frees one from the ordinary, mundane parameters of consciousness to reveal the true nature of existence.

When one has awakened to the essence of existence, when the eye of Truth has opened, one knows that there is only Allah, the Living, the Ever-Continuing. The awakened being exists in this life by a direct, perceptual recognition of the living. Those who truly seek Allah will heed the message that the purpose of this existence is to polish and purify the limited self (*nafs*) so as to be able to recognize the reflection of Allah's unlimited Hand behind everything.

The record 'of what they have sent ahead, and the traces they have left behind' refers to people's actions. Every moment contains traces of the past, projecting them toward the future. Our present actions will continue to have an effect on us, both good and bad. On the other hand, every moment is a fresh moment. The sincere performance of the ritual ablution (*wudu*) in praise of Allah and in gratitude for His boundless mercy creates a state in which we are present as witnesses in that moment. Allah says in a divinely revealed tradition (*hadith qudsi*): 'The heavens and earth do not contain Me but the heart of the believer contains Me.'

'And their traces': everything is a trace. We ourselves are traces of the One Reality. Everywhere we look and in everything we see there is a trace or sign of Allah. All has come from Allah, all is absorbed in Allah, and all is sustained by Allah. Everything is saturated with divine essence.

The Arabic word translated as 'traces' in this verse is *āthār*, meaning 'what one leaves behind', from the verb meaning 'to draw, effect, to influence'. Through our actions we leave many traces of our passage through life, some of which will enhance other people's passages. If, however, we leave crooked tracks, then whoever comes along behind us will have to cope with them. One description of the men of Allah is that when they leave their places there is nothing other than the smell of sweet perfume.

We each reproduce the Book which is traced within. The more faithful and submissive we are the truer the outer reproduction of the inner original trace. A physical analogy may be sought in the process of holography, which produces a photographic record called a hologram. Any piece of the hologram will reconstruct the entire image. Similarly, man's self (*nafs*) is a 'trace', a part of the one Reality.

'We have recorded everything in a clear Book': everything in the existence of each one of us is already being counted, measured and recorded in a book. Nothing is lost, everything has its place of manifestation, recording and recycling. Nothing can escape; it may metamorphose from one form to another, from living to dead, from energy to matter, but nothing is ever lost in this cosmos. One of the dilemmas of today's scientists is the concept of limited space, for in human knowledge and understanding of physical phenomena and cosmology one must assume a limitation of some kind. The question is: 'If space is totally limited, what is behind it?' The concept of the limited cannot exist without the concomitant notion, or underlying ground, of the unlimited! Whatever one observes and experiences is within the bounds of the limited, but the limited can only be meaningful if it is encompassed, engulfed and given definition by the unlimited.

Everything is accounted for in 'a clear Book' (*fi 'imām mubīn*). This could refer to the Qur'an itself or it could also refer to a man of knowledge, for the word translated as 'Book' is *'imām* which means a leader. In regard to this, the Prophet said in a tradition: 'You have not died the death befitting a Muslim or a believer (*mu'min*) if you do not know the leader (*Imām*) of your time.' And the men of Allah say: 'If you do not have a man of Allah as your master, the *Shaytān* will be your master.' Another interpretation of the 'clear Book' is that this also refers to 'Alī ibn Abi Tālib, for in a most famous tradition the Prophet Muhammad said: 'I am the city of knowledge, and 'Ali is its gate.'

The 'clear Book' also refers to the 'well-guarded tablet' (*al-lawh al-mahfūz*), which provides the creational blueprint. This meaning is very clearly brought out in *Sūrat al-Baqarah* (Chapter of The Cow), when Allah tells Adam to inform the angels of the 'names' of all He has taught him. He was ordered to do this because he had within him that dimension which encapsulated all knowledges, whereas the angelic powers, resembling beams of energy, had only a restricted and clearly defined channel. Before this, Allah had informed the angels that He was going to create a representative (*khalīfah*) on earth. Since the angels knew that the power of Allah comprised both creation and destruction, they complained that this creature was going to create havoc and destruction while they continuously glorified Allah. At this point, Allah commanded Adam to reveal his knowledge: 'Tell them the names, give them the knowledge you have!' In this state, Adam reflected his original divine nature (*fitra matbū'ah*), the pure Adamic blueprint. When the angels saw that this knowledge actually reflected the knowledge of the Creator, they submitted to Adam. His knowledge represented all the various existential situations possible in the total spectrum of creation. Real knowledge is divine knowledge from Allah. Thus Adam, the original being, as the receptacle of such knowledge, was also the 'clear Book' (*imām mubīn*).

Creation began from an eternal sea of motionlessness, where no phenomena were exhibited. There were no Attributes, only pure Essence — Essential Being. From that Essence arose power and through power the creation, including the creation of beings. From that progression arose the capacities of sight, speech and the other faculties of the human being.

Throughout life, man performs visible actions which are preceded by mental processes and which are expressed in speech. Among Islamic traditions the following is found: 'We are a people who do what we say, say what we mean, and do not say everything that comes to mind.' This means that one speaks the truth and acts according to it. The outer aspect of action is guided and given shape by knowledge of the outer Law (*Sharī'ah*), and the inner aspect of it by one's intention, which is the intangible, propelling truth (*haqīqah*). What we are presently writing on our biographical tablets by the pen of our actions will be left behind as traces (*athār*), for actions include speech.

The end is in the beginning. One's spirit (*rūh*) will continue to resonate with the vibration of its condition. The experience of the next life is based upon the final condition of the spirit at the time of its departure from the physical vehicle of the body. If it is in complete submission, in true Islam, it will enjoy a state whose quality accords with that, but if it is full of arrogance and negative characteristics, then that is what its state will reflect. For this reason, we say: 'Say only One, see only One, be only One!' Shaykh 'Abd al-Salam ibn Mashish, a great Moroccan man of Allah, said: 'O Allah, rescue me from the mire of the knowledge of unity and drown me in the source of the unitive ocean.'

وَٱضۡرِبۡ لَهُم مَّثَلًا أَصۡحَـٰبَ ٱلۡقَرۡيَةِ إِذۡ جَآءَهَا ٱلۡمُرۡسَلُونَ ﴿١٣﴾

13. And strike an analogy for them, the people of the town, when the messengers came to it.

This verse is an example of the continuing, compassionate lordship (*rubūbiyyah*) from One Who is constantly sending man reminders to awaken him to his true nature as a worshipper of Truth. Having been given the universal message of warning against wrong actions, actions that lead to the chains of arrogance, Allah says: 'Strike an analogy for them', as though the words themselves were used to cause a shock of awakening,

'Give them the example (*mathal*) of the people of the village', refers to when the Prophet Jesus sent some of his disciples as messengers to them, out of his abundant, overflowing love, to show them that the whole of the way is about submission: 'Come to submission, the gateway of Islam, All who have a heavy weight upon your shoulders, give it up, and be free! Throw away the chains of attachments, expectations, vanity, fears, anxieties and insecurities. Put on the garlands of inner freedom and self-abandonment by translating wrong intentions into good intentions, and by bringing good intentions out into correct actions.'

Lordship is perpetual. This is why we say that Islam will prevail, Islam meaning submission to inner evolution and

awakening. Biologically, everyone began from a tiny cell and
ended up in this most complex form of a human being, walking
upright on two legs with senses bringing awareness and limbs
which act and move. Collectively as a species, humankind has
also undergone, since its first appearance, a few mutations in
its development along a certain progression; we do not know
precisely how this has taken place, but obviously there was an
origin to it, so we must know.

As far as Allah is concerned, it is 'Be! And it is' (*kun
fayakūn*). Time cannot be experienced without its instantaneous
antithesis, non-time; thus, 'Be! And it is.' The backdrop
screen on which the film appears is immobile but everything
reflected on it moves. Movement could not be recognized
unless the background was still. Conversely, absolute, eternal
stillness could not be experienced by us unless mobility was
superimposed on it. Man is the interspace (*barzakh*) between
the Seen and the Unseen, for he encompasses both: 'The
heavens and earth do not contain Me but the heart of the
believer (*mu'min*) contains Me.'

إِذْ أَرْسَلْنَآ إِلَيْهِمُ ٱثْنَيْنِ فَكَذَّبُوهُمَا فَعَزَّزْنَا بِثَالِثٍ فَقَالُوٓاْ إِنَّآ إِلَيْكُم مُّرْسَلُونَ ﴿١٤﴾

14. When We sent to them two, they rejected them both, so We strengthened [them] with a third, and they said: Truly, we are messengers sent to you!

This is an example of the affliction other messengers had
to bear. Their task was to call people to the path of Allah
through submission and trust, giving a clear warning as well,
about the consequences of their actions. Often, however, their
exhortations fell on deaf ears. Prophets throughout the ages
have had few true followers.

Two messengers were not sufficient for the city of Antioch,
so Allah reinforced them with a third, the great Unitarian
(*muwahhid*) and the close disciple of Jesus, Simon al-Safi. In the
same way as these three messengers were sent to this specific

city, so too do we receive the message within our own inner
'city', for within each one of us is encompassed the essence of
everything we observe, measure and comprehend outwardly.

قَالُوا مَآ أَنتُمۡ إِلَّا بَشَرٌ مِّثۡلُنَا وَمَآ أَنزَلَ ٱلرَّحۡمَٰنُ مِن شَىۡءٍ إِنۡ أَنتُمۡ إِلَّا تَكۡذِبُونَ ﴿١٥﴾

15. They said: You are only mortals like us. The
Beneficent has revealed nothing. You are only lying!

The people of the city who were in a state of denial expected
some odd phenomena, something strange, shocking and out
of the ordinary, something miraculous. So they protested
to the messengers, saying: 'But you are only people like us,
how can we take you seriously, how do we know that you are
messengers of the Beneficent? You must be lying! We see you
as mere human beings, so what qualifies you to say what you
are saying?' They could not accept that these messengers were
representing the Prophet Jesus. Jesus' message was to abandon
oneself, possess nothing of this world, have nothing but love
for others and Allah will fulfill his undertaking and promise,
and   take you into His mercy, if only you will let yourself
be taken! This was from the generosity and greatness of Jesus
whose message was the same as all the major prophets of
Allah.

The Prophet Muhammad would not allow people to place
him on a pedestal nor let them think of him as a supernatural
being. He would always remind them that he was a human being
like anyone else, except for his high intention and revealed
knowledge, that he ate meat and was born of a woman, all
so that his people might not go astray. He was only a true
messenger carrying and relaying the message, the meaning of
which cannot be dissociated from the source in its totality.
Once one has grasped it and tasted it, one has it! Like the very
thin, barely visible crescent of a new moon which appears
elusively in the twilight sky, at first it cannot be discerned, but
once one has seen it, one has experienced it, and once one

has seen one crescent one has seen all crescents. Such vision requires a narrowing of the focus, not a widening.

The path toward the knowledge of Allah is narrow, not broad. That is why we often find the men of Allah supplicating: 'O Allah, give us the narrow way, give us a single point which is the whole point,' A man of real submission is absolutely, fanatically single-minded in his quest. He desires only Allah and obtains his goal through concentrated, total submission. The lovers of Allah who burn with intense longing are willing to abandon everything for that goal, and nothing else matters. The beginning is trust in the Messenger and in the message.

$$\text{قَالُوا۟ رَبُّنَا يَعْلَمُ إِنَّآ إِلَيْكُمْ لَمُرْسَلُونَ ﴿١٦﴾}$$

16. They said: Our Lord knows that we are truly messengers sent to you.

Here the Arabic word *Rabb* for 'Lord', is used because in Arabic it describes 'that entity which brings one up to one's fullest potential'. Thus they declare that they have been raised to that higher state and are qualified to carry Jesus' message. All they could say was, 'Our Lord (*Rabb*), our Sustainer by Whose power of knowledge we have reached that higher knowledge, He Who is bringing everyone in His creation to a point of fulfilled potential, knows that we have only come to you as messengers. We but repeat the one eternal tune.'

$$\text{وَمَا عَلَيْنَآ إِلَّا ٱلْبَلَٰغُ ٱلْمُبِينُ ﴿١٧﴾}$$

17. We have no obligation except the clear deliverance [of the message].

The messengers came with the obvious news, the clear signs, but the people were at a loss, veiled, and therefore doomed. Their actions had chained and disconnected them from Reality over such a long period of time that they were no longer able to see their situation clearly. But the messengers delivering the prophetic message saw it and where it was leading them. There is an aspect of cognition which does not easily recognize change over time unless it is dramatic.

The messenger is only responsible for the straightforward conveyance of the message. The people of Antioch resisted the message, for they were content with their situation as it was. Man's attempt to fixate on what is around him is the result of his nature as a creature of habit. For this reason, the men of Allah break norms. The man on the path to Allah recognizes the extent to which he is chained by his expectation of the repetitive patterns he is used to, and how much a creature and virtual prisoner of his ingrained habits he really is. Naturally, when slaves of habits are confronted with dynamic submission to reality, they find themselves threatened and react defensively.

قَالُوٓا۟ إِنَّا تَطَيَّرْنَا بِكُمْ لَئِن لَّمْ تَنتَهُوا۟ لَنَرْجُمَنَّكُمْ وَلَيَمَسَّنَّكُم مِّنَّا عَذَابٌ أَلِيمٌ ﴿١٨﴾

18. They said: Surely, we augur evil from you. If you do not stop we shall stone you, and a painful punishment will afflict you from our hands.

Conditioned by living in a mostly desert, sparse terrain and environment, the people of the Middle East were acutely sensitive to their surroundings. The appearance of various animals, especially birds, was often regarded as omens. What the people were saying to these messengers was that their presence was a bad omen and their continued presentation of the message would be ill received.

قَالُوا۟ طَـٰٓئِرُكُم مَّعَكُمْ أَئِن ذُكِّرْتُم بَلْ أَنتُمْ قَوْمٌ مُّسْرِفُونَ ﴿١٩﴾

19. They said: Your evil omens are with yourselves. [Deem ye this an evil omen] if you are admonished? Nay, you are a prodigal people [transgressing all bounds].

The messengers replied, declaring that they, the people of

Antioch, were the source of their own evil auspices on account of their actions. If only one could become aware that this 'bad omen' or sign has come about as result of one's denial of the truth, one would be free. What interferes with one's receptivity is having already gone too far, exceeding the boundaries of what is useful and needed — having been, as this verse indicates, *musrif*, i.e, prodigal. The messengers tell the people, 'You have gone beyond the boundaries of the correct behavior that is conducive to apprehending the One Reality so how can you possibly remember? This dead-end situation is a result of your own extravagant ignorance.' This is the veil created by replacing the real or practical with concepts and expectations.

The people referred to in this verse rejected the messenger's criticism because they did not want to be shaken out of their lethargy. The prophetic message causes trouble. Its purpose is to shake people out of their complacent illusions. Allah is not wasteful. He would not send a messenger to people who are already single-mindedly worshipping Him. A prophet or messenger is never sent except to remind people of Reality. Thus Allah says: 'That you may warn a people whose fathers were not warned.'

One of the insights afforded by *Surat Yā Sīn* is that one brings about one's own doom. By thoughts, intentions and actions we each dictate our own future. The true believer's intentions are directed exclusively toward the abandonment of the lower self, because he has found that salvation cannot be had otherwise. He has been bewildered enough by running between *Safa*, and *Marwah*, the two hills in Mecca between which the *Hajj* pilgrims run back and forth, symbolizing the nature of worldly pursuit from one thing or event to another. Going in circles around the *Ka'bah* has made him dizzy, so he kisses the Black Stone and is annihilated, after which he is allowed the two cycles of prayer at the station of Abraham, where he has surrendered in prostration. Then, and only then, is he authorized to act, understanding that he is responsible for his existing situation, the author of his own biography by the translation of his intentions into thoughts and actions.

Creation is a symbiotic system set up with perfect justice (balance). The Qur'an is revealed for man to understand the inherent code of justice and the divine balance of existence in every case and at all times. Only man himself may dictate what is going to happen to him by his own intentions and resultant actions. However, the duration of life throbbing in his heart is not in his hands. What man puts forth will have an immediate result according to the laws that govern existence. When one trusts that the existential situations of creation are perfectly interconnected, all operating according to divine laws, one will see the Names and Attributes of Allah in creation. This will lead one to contemplation of Allah, removed from time and space.

$$\text{وَجَآءَ مِنْ أَقْصَا ٱلْمَدِينَةِ رَجُلٌ يَسْعَىٰ قَالَ يَٰقَوْمِ ٱتَّبِعُوا۟ ٱلْمُرْسَلِينَ ﴿٢٠﴾}$$

20. And from the farthest part of the city a man came running who said: O my people, follow the messengers.

A man among the people of Antioch had grasped the message, for he had heard the voice from the outside and recognized the truth of it within himself. He came rushing forth in support of the truth.

Coming 'from the other end of the city', suddenly there is a readiness to listen. Historically, this man was Habib al-Najjar. He came beseeching the people to follow the messengers and their message. Each one of our inner cities has its Habib, a voice which says: 'Look, this is true!' This is deep resonance, not memory recalling what one heard yesterday, but remembering what is written in one's original nature (*fitrah*). Its analogy is the echo-sounder or sonar used by certain deep-water fish, listening to what is beyond time, that which is already contained within us, the laws of Allah. 'The heavens and earth do not contain

Me, but the heart of the believer contains Me.'

Access to that innermost knowledge is through the sound of deepest intuition welling up from within one, but because so much debris chokes the well of knowledge hardly anything gets through.

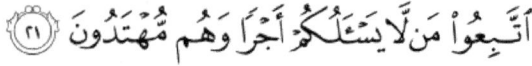

اَتَّبِعُواْ مَن لَّا يَسْئَلُكُمْ أَجْرًا وَهُم مُّهْتَدُونَ ﴿٢١﴾

21. Follow him who asks no reward of you, and they are rightly guided.

The man who received the message had no option but to come forth and attempt to share it. 'Follow the ones who are trying to guide you,' he says, and then he defines who is a true messenger. The first condition is that he does not ask or expect any reward or recompense for his teaching. When someone asks for a reward, expecting personal gain or recognition, this means he is not free from desire and self-image. The second criterion of a true messenger is that he brings forth guidance that is clearly recognizable to every sincere person from his or her own personal standpoint; or, to paraphrase a prophetic tradition, he speaks to each person in a way that he can understand.

One must be totally efficient to follow the path of Reality, and efficiency can only occur where there is total and spontaneous awareness. Is one doing the right thing at the right time in the right manner in the right place to the right person? If not, then one will not be efficient but wasteful, and that is ignorance.

Throughout history, true spiritual teaching has always been free from undue stress or anxiety. It is up to the people who are receiving the teaching to give time, service or money to show their gratitude outwardly to their teacher. One will never detect any expectations from a truly spiritual teacher for outer rewards, because his teaching is the reward. In fact, there are examples when the real teacher of Truth pays those who come to receive the teaching.

The highest reward for delivering the message is the message itself, passing it on, singing it fully. The man from the furthest part of the city, and likewise the voice in our heart says:

وَمَا لِيَ لَآ أَعْبُدُ ٱلَّذِى فَطَرَنِى وَإِلَيْهِ تُرْجَعُونَ ﴿٢٢﴾

22. And why should I not worship Him Who brought me into existence, and to Him you will return?

The word translated as 'brought into existence' (*fatara*), in this verse, means 'to break or split open', hence also 'to create', and is related to 'original nature' (*fitrah*). Man possesses an original nature, or *fitrah*, as an echo in his heart of the original burst of creation, the first light bursting forth. Creation is forever breaking open, exploding and expanding from the Unseen into the visible world. Whatever expands must also eventually collapse. The Big Bang will reach its outer limits and then return. Every system has its boundary and the opposite, for everything in existence has a destiny. Time-space curves in upon itself.

To worship means to adore. It is an outer manifestation of inner love. Before our creation we had no idea that there was existence, no idea that a world existed. So the voice says: 'How may I orientate myself toward any other than the One Who caused me to be?'

We are the products of cause. Whatever comes to us, whether knowledge, possessions or events, comes to us from a cause emanating from an unbroken, continuous source — a stream, a dynamic effulgence manifesting as time and space. Allah may therefore be described in scientific terms as the Non-Dimensional Timeless, for He is beyond anything one can ascribe to Him.

The voice says: 'If I take anything other than the One-and-Only Reality as a god, I am in obvious error.' One must trust in Lordship (*Rubūbīyyah*), in that Attribute whose purpose is to bring one to full awakening at the right time and in the right manner. One must trust that even if one is in darkness, it is for one's own benefit, for should one come to know something before its time the knowledge may be in imbalance and subject to abuse. When the mercy (*rahmah*) of Allah descends on a person in spiritual retreat (*khalwah*), it is nothing other than seeing and knowing the most obvious. The obvious becomes obvious, nothing more. Nothing else happens. If one expects anything else, the expectation itself becomes another barrier. There is no wanting if one is in a state of self-abandonment. For this reason, the man of Allah says that the man who is ready for spiritual retreat is the man who is completely cornered, who sees no way out, who is finished with desires and ambitions. When he tastes death, he can begin again. His end has become his beginning just as Allah has neither beginning nor end — 'and to Him you shall return'.

ءَأَتَّخِذُ مِن دُونِهِۦٓ ءَالِهَةً إِن يُرِدۡنِ ٱلرَّحۡمَٰنُ بِضُرٍّ لَّا تُغۡنِ عَنِّي شَفَٰعَتُهُمۡ شَيۡـًٔا وَلَا يُنقِذُونِ ﴿٢٣﴾

23. Shall I take other gods besides Him? If the Beneficent should intend some adversity for me, of no use whatever will be their intercession, nor can they deliver me.

Taking other than the One-and-Only Creator Who brought about one's creation and sustains it by His love could never bring about intercession (*shafā'ah*), for the boundaries of Allah's mercy have been transgressed. The verb '*shafa'a*', from which the word 'intercession' (*shafā'ah*) is derived, means 'to double, attach or enclose', implying solace and comfort that comes from proximity. Seeking intercession is reassurance and guidance. When the boundaries of the Beneficent are transgressed, how can His intercession possibly take place?

$$\text{إِنِّىٓ إِذًا لَّفِى ضَلَلٍ مُّبِينٍ (٢٤)}$$

24. In that case I would truly be in clear error.

If one were to worship anything other than the One God Who creates and nurtures, however attractive or seemingly powerful, then one would be obviously misguided and in evident loss.

$$\text{إِنِّىٓ ءَامَنتُ بِرَبِّكُمْ فَٱسْمَعُونِ (٢٥)}$$

25. Surely, I believe in your Lord, so listen to me.

The voice, that original nature (*fitrah*) echoing from the other end of the city, echoes from the depths of the heart and says: 'I believe, I have submitted, I have trusted knowledge of your Lord. I know the Lord's affair is to sustain me, to open me to my full potential at the right time. So hear me, hear this voice!' That faint, distant voice is of great subtlety: it must call out to be heard.

$$\text{قِيلَ ٱدْخُلِ ٱلْجَنَّةَ قَالَ يَلَيْتَ قَوْمِى يَعْلَمُونَ (٢٦)}$$

26. It was said: Enter the Garden. He said: O would that my people knew!

The word *jannah* used for 'Garden' means one cannot see the ground for the lush denseness of foliage. It is a secret garden, hidden and quiet. The word indicates a state. Arabic, as the language for the final divine revelation, is a language of contrast arid duality stemming from oneness: the garden inside, the desert outside; Islam inside, denial of Reality (*kufr*) outside; peace inside, war outside. Entry to the state of the Garden is only by leaving behind all disturbances at its gate: 'Enter in peace from Us, and blessings upon you' (11: 48).

For the one who is guided to Allah, the Eternal, the Hereafter (*Akhirah*) is near, and the waiting in the grave assumes the condition of the Garden. The Day of Reckoning shrinks to the instant present, when one sees the ultimate reward of eternal bliss. The voice in time echoes the experience of that timeless state, saying: 'O would that my people knew!'

Clearly, this verse means that one who has submitted to the Lord is promised the eternal Garden, meaning the state of joy and bliss, for how could that person have recognized the truth of the Garden unless he had already begun to experience it?

'O would that my people knew!' he exclaims, expressing his indescribable joy upon tasting this knowledge of the smooth entry into the Garden, the knowledge of submission to the message and of moving along the path of unity (*tawhīd*), the knowledge that there is only Allah.

$$\text{بِمَا غَفَرَ لِى رَبِّى وَجَعَلَنِى مِنَ ٱلْمُكْرَمِينَ ﴿٢٧﴾}$$

27. Of what my Lord has forgiven me and placed me among those who are honored.

The man of the city, the man of the heart who received the message, is able to recognize the great honor (*karam*), the great exaltation he has been accorded by the generosity of Allah because of his self-abandonment. The Arabic word *ghafara*, translated here as 'forgiven', also means 'to cover, protect, shield'. Forgiveness means rendering oneself safe from the results of past wrong actions or future desires and expectations.

$$\text{﴿ وَمَآ أَنزَلْنَا عَلَىٰ قَوْمِهِۦ مِنۢ بَعْدِهِۦ مِن جُندٍ مِّنَ ٱلسَّمَآءِ وَمَا كُنَّا مُنزِلِينَ ﴿٢٨﴾}$$

28. And We did not send down upon his people after him armies from heaven, nor do We ever send down.

The obvious meaning of this verse is that Allah would not send down 'armies' after the death of this man, who confirmed the truth of the messengers and was a living proof of them. In this case, 'armies' (*jund*) means 'angelic forces accompanying each other'. A soldier in an army is constrained, for he only carries out orders from a higher command.

The verse also explains the meaning of the messenger's statement to the people of Antioch: 'Your evil omen is with you.' Upon delivery of the truth, Allah does not suddenly afflict a people with supernatural phenomena, 'nor do We ever send down'. It is by one's own transgressions that one's doom is sealed.

$$\text{إِن كَانَتْ إِلَّا صَيْحَةً وَاحِدَةً فَإِذَا هُمْ خَامِدُونَ} \quad (٢٩)$$

29. It was but a single shout, and they were extinguished.

When the end comes, whether the beginning of the final cosmic Big Bang, the downfall of a culture, or one's individual death, it comes as a single, decisive event. In the same way that creation was shocked into existence it will be shocked out of it again. The Big Bang will become the big collapse. From a microcosmic point of view, as well as a collective, macrocosmic point of view, the whole cosmos will be shocked into extinction, to return whence it came.

The 'single shout' could also refer to the shock of awakening, when one's individual, motivating will is extinguished. Man has been given the ability to choose and act towards inner freedom by means of self-knowledge or to choose and act towards inner enslavement by denial of Reality and ignorance. There is no freedom from destiny. The only freedom one really possesses is one's attitude towards destiny. Provided one's attitude is based on submission, from which comes knowledge that is useful to one at any particular time, one is free. The single shout heralds the end of any possibility of taking action. After death, the spirit (*rūh*) continues transmitting the state it was in at death, like a radio eternally transmitting whatever station it is tuned to.

$$\text{يَٰحَسْرَةً عَلَى ٱلْعِبَادِ مَا يَأْتِيهِم مِّن رَّسُولٍ إِلَّا كَانُوا۟ بِهِۦ يَسْتَهْزِءُونَ ﴿٣٠﴾}$$

30. Alas for the slaves! Never does a messenger come to them but they mock him.

Allah calls everyone a slave (*'abd*), or bondsman. Everyone is enslaved in some way because no one can escape death or the fact that one must breathe and eat. Each one of us has tasted both the Fire and the Garden; these are conditions already experienced in the physical realm. The purpose of the path of Islam is to demonstrate the boundaries, the transgression of which will only bring affliction, agony and trouble, now and in the future.

In many chapters of the Qur'an we find such verses that try to increase our yearning (*himmah*) for the truth. People who refuse to acknowledge their slavery outwardly by putting their heads on the ground in prostration (*sajdah*), and inwardly by seeking reality (*haqiqah*) are cheating themselves, for every time a messenger comes to them, they abuse and mock (*yastahzi'un*) both him and the message of Truth that he bears. Mockery is one of the worst human characteristics described in the Qur'an. It is an arrogant and desperate expression of the lower ego and proof that the ego is solid and dominating. By mocking someone we assert our own 'righteousness' and their 'wrongdoing'. Self-congratulation clearly shows the limitation of one's knowledge and, therefore, one's weakness.

Allah explains in the Qur'an that those who mock receive the worst of afflictions, both outwardly and inwardly. Do not look down on the creation, for the tiniest of creatures, the germs, are ultimately one's most potent adversaries. A small stone which you consider of no account may actually crack your skull open. One must not treat with contempt what one does not understand but preserve one's energy for moving in a positive direction towards the increase of self-knowledge. Mockery dissipates energy, while the path of Islam, the path of positive being, preserves energy for success.

The only purpose of the path of submission is to bypass the ego, the illusory 'I'. When the ego is extinguished, then the opening to Reality, which is already there, appears.

أَلَمْ يَرَوْا كَمْ أَهْلَكْنَا قَبْلَهُم مِّنَ ٱلْقُرُونِ أَنَّهُمْ إِلَيْهِمْ لَا يَرْجِعُونَ ﴿٣١﴾

31. Have they not seen how many generations We destroyed before them? Indeed, they will not return to them.

Those individuals, villages, cultures or nations that have not been travelling in the direction of self-enlightenment, along the path of abandonment and submission to the Reality from which they have never been separate, will fall by the wayside. This verse asks us to reflect upon how many people were brought to naught and annihilated. One is no longer able to connect with, or return to, them. One's ancestors or previous cultures are gone forever, leaving scarcely a trace behind.

Man naturally becomes accustomed to his environment, wanting to preserve his outward routine and habits. Creation however, is dynamic and ever-changing, but underlying the existential turmoil is that echo of foreverness, of timelessness, which explains why we should be attracted to the continuity of routine. Man is basically a creature of habit. Even biologically all the cells of the body seek to continue. We want to live forever because of our love for Him Who is forever.

Everything in existence is permeated and encompassed by Allah's creational laws. His Essence cannot be comprehended by that which flows in the creational stream and is sustained by the power of the stream itself. How can the leaf understand the nature of the river upon which it is floating? Only if it will give up its 'leafness', dissolve into and unify with the current, can it resonate or reflect the nature of the stream which urges it along on its journey.

$$\text{وَإِن كُلٌّ لَّمَّا جَمِيعٌ لَّدَيْنَا مُحْضَرُونَ ۝}$$

32. But all of them shall certainly be brought before Us.

There is only the Presence of Lordship (*al – Hadrah al-Rabbāniyyah*). Everything is already in the presence of the Lord. Full awareness of this would allow us to see nothing but Lordship, nothing but the Merciful present in everything. The choice is up to us.

$$\text{وَءَايَةٌ لَّهُمُ ٱلْأَرْضُ ٱلْمَيْتَةُ أَحْيَيْنَٰهَا وَأَخْرَجْنَا مِنْهَا حَبًّا فَمِنْهُ يَأْكُلُونَ ۝}$$

33. And a sign to them is the dead earth. We enliven it and bring forth from it grain so they may eat of it.

This is the first of nine different signs that are put forth here, one after the other, so that one may gain greater knowledge about the laws at work in this existential reality. There is an order in which these things appear and a reason for that order. Qur'anic references usually begin with the gross and lead to the more subtle.

Everything is an indication of Allah. Wherever one looks there is a sign, frequently to be found in opposites. One sign is the earth which was previously dead and then made fertile. The earth's rhythm is cyclical, and by it its inhabitants are sustained. The multiplicity of events, which together form one ecosystem, are signs indicating the One Sustainer behind them.

We are reminded here that the earth after its creation was dead. It cooled down from its molten state and then afterwards came the rain and oceans and lakes were formed. From the water, as well from the soil of the earth, came life forms. Geology has determined that this process took several hundred million years.

The Arabic word *habb*, here translated as grain, also means seed. For the seed to fulfill its potential as a plant or tree it must burst open beyond its boundaries, annihilating itself in a completely transformative process.

وَجَعَلْنَا فِيهَا جَنَّـٰتٍ مِّن نَّخِيـلٍ وَأَعْنَـٰبٍ وَفَجَّرْنَا فِيهَا مِنَ ٱلْعُيُونِ ﴿٣٤﴾

34. And We make therein gardens of palm-trees and grapevines, and We cause springs to flow forth in it.

'Gardens' (*jannāt*) refers either to a physical garden or an inner, unseen Garden. Usually, when the Qur'an talks about gardens that are fed by underground springs, it implies the 'state' of being in a garden, the state of inner tranquility, peace, satisfaction, complete contentment and joy.

After the creation of the earth and its enlivening, gardens containing palm-trees and grapevines were among the different types of garden that were created. The date-palm is a most ancient and evolved plant form, standing almost at the boundary between the plant and the animal kingdoms. The date-palm has a heart. If one tries to drown the tree, it will die when the water goes above a certain height, above the heart. Popular opinion holds that it has the rudiments of consciousness. A common practice in the old palm groves of the east is to threaten a female plant if it does not produce dates after several years. Date palms have gender; the female of the species is pollinated by the male palm, thereby producing its fruit.

'And We cause springs to flow forth in it.' The word for 'springs' (*'uyūn*) is the plural of *'ayn*, which also means 'source.' Thus another meaning related to this verse is that this state of paradise flows or streams forth from the source.

$$\text{لِيَأْكُلُوا مِن ثَمَرِهِ وَمَا عَمِلَتْهُ أَيْدِيهِمْ ۖ أَفَلَا يَشْكُرُونَ ﴿٣٥﴾}$$

35. That they may eat of its fruit, and their hands made it not. Will they not then give thanks?

There are many verses in the Qur'an which can be read in more than one way, each making equal sense; this is one of the unfathomable glories of the Qur'an. One meaning of this verse is that they eat of its fruits and also of 'what their hands make', implying the products and by-products, such as dried fruits, syrups and the like, which are made from these fruits. Another implication is that man's hands have not independently accomplished the creation of his sustenance, so should he not be grateful for the generosity of this garden?

Gardens on this earth are a prelude to, and a foretaste of, that final Garden, as if people are being gradually introduced to the final Garden while in this world. The same is true of agitated, fire-like conditions and other similar situations. They are also a gradual preparation for the Fire in the next realm of consciousness. The state of the Garden is so elevated and pure that it necessitates preparation beforehand, otherwise that full state of bliss in the Hereafter would be unattainable. Consciousness follows a continuum both forward and backward. One step leads to another.

Joy, contentment and correct actions lead to the Garden, while misery, agitation and wrong actions lead to the final unending state of the Fire. The door of entry into the Garden is gratitude (*shukr*), which brings about freedom from expectations and desires, opening the heart to increase in faith (*īmān*) and the light (*nūr*) of knowledge by which one can see Allah's manifestations in the creations.

سُبْحَنَ ٱلَّذِى خَلَقَ ٱلْأَزْوَجَ كُلَّهَا مِمَّا تُنْبِتُ ٱلْأَرْضُ وَمِنْ أَنفُسِهِمْ وَمِمَّا لَا يَعْلَمُونَ ﴿٣٦﴾

36. Glory be to Him Who created in pairs all things that grow in the earth, and pairs of their own kind, and of what they do not know.

After gratitude (*shukr*) comes a state of glorification, for gratitude and abandonment naturally lead to a state of exaltation, free from the association of the characteristics of any created being with Allah. Everything in the earth, as well as within man's inward and outward domain, is based on pairs (*azwāj*), on complementary opposites. He Who created all pairs is not tarnished by their duality. He, Allah, is far removed from need, yet all His creation are in need of Him.

This glorification is based on the apprehension of the miraculous, creational state of affairs. The entire planet consists of opposites, yet the transcendence of the creational situation depends on joining these opposites, on unification.

وَءَايَةٌ لَّهُمُ ٱلَّيْلُ نَسْلَخُ مِنْهُ ٱلنَّهَارَ فَإِذَا هُم مُّظْلِمُونَ ﴿٣٧﴾

37. And a sign to them is the night. We strip from it the day, then they are in darkness.

The Arabic word translated as 'strip' is *salakha* which usually refers to 'skinning', inferring that an outer layer exists over a body or entity. From a figurative point of view the darkness of night may refer to the obscurity of ignorance or loss. One meaning derived from this verse is that what underlies creation is non-existence, complete stillness, non-creation. Stripping off the day implies that the day is a skin upon the night, the main body being the night. Creation rests upon cosmic darkness, covered only by an effulgent veneer of light. Sunlight, in fact, does not penetrate the earth very deeply, but just penetrates the earth's crust slightly. Everything below remains in darkness. Basically, though, the nature of light is constant agitation of photons or waves, whereas darkness is a state of silence and stillness. Night therefore echoes the pre-creational state.

Before we can see the light of knowledge, we have to come to the surface of ourselves, we must emerge from the dark corridors of the ego-self (*nafs*) and its illusions. We do not belong to the world; we are in it but not of it. We experience the ego, but that is not our essential reality. Once the light of the higher self is fully experienced, the joy of self-awakening has begun.

The sincere seeker must challenge the Qur'an. What does it mean? 'And a sign for them is the night. We strip from it the day!' Here is an astonishing statement. Do not be frightened of it. Challenge it with sincerity and humility and, while in darkness, the light of Islam will shine and suffuse man's consciousness.

وَٱلشَّمْسُ تَجْرِى لِمُسْتَقَرٍّ لَّهَا ذَٰلِكَ تَقْدِيرُ ٱلْعَزِيزِ ٱلْعَلِيمِ ﴿٣٨﴾

38. And the sun runs on to a term appointed for it. That is the measured decree of the Mighty, the All-Knowing,

Creation is based upon opposites, and everything operates according to a measure. Everything moves along an appointed course in its passage through the time-space dimension. This is the decree of the Mighty (*al-'Azīz*), the All-Knowing (*al-'Alīm*). Everything is decreed according to a knowledge programmed within it that is from the knowledge of the All-Knowing, brought into manifestation by His might. It is cosmos, not chaos, and it is subtle. The Arabic word *'azīz*, translated as 'mighty' also means 'rare, precious, difficult of access'.

When a verse ends with any of the Divine Names of Allah, we usually find a direct relationship between the Names and the verse itself. These Names are used to unlock and open the inner meaning of the verse. Conversely, the description of events in the verse indicates the meaning of the Name.

Here the Name 'the Mighty' (*al-ʿAzīz*) refers to the sun, and the All-knowing (*al-ʿAlīm*) refers to its destiny, its calculation. The continuous, self-detonating, hydrogen-to-helium fusion process, which goes on in the sun, is indeed mighty and hard of access, and the measured decree which keeps the whole system going could only have been set up by One who is All-Knowing.

وَٱلۡقَمَرَ قَدَّرۡنَٰهُ مَنَازِلَ حَتَّىٰ عَادَ كَٱلۡعُرۡجُونِ ٱلۡقَدِيمِ ﴿٣٩﴾

39. And the moon, We have appointed stages for it, until it returns like an old shriveled palm-leaf.

The moon also has been programmed by the decree to go through its various phases, without which life and the ecological balance of the earth could not continue. The moon and its light have an enormous effect on plants and their cycles of growth, upon the tides, mankind and all living beings. The cycle of the moon — the waxing and waning — symbolizes the creational cycle of rising up to reach full effulgence then diminishing and dying down. Everything in creation is cyclical, including man, who moves from a position of weakness to physical strength, and then back again through weakness to death.

لَا ٱلشَّمۡسُ يَنۢبَغِي لَهَآ أَن تُدۡرِكَ ٱلۡقَمَرَ وَلَا ٱلَّيۡلُ سَابِقُ ٱلنَّهَارِ وَكُلٌّ فِي فَلَكٖ يَسۡبَحُونَ ﴿٤٠﴾

40. The sun does not overtake the moon, nor does the night outstrip the day. Each follows its orbital course.

Every entity has its pre-destined, pre-measured course. The night will never overtake the day. Each planet is aswim in its circular, repetitive orbital pattern, moving according to the laws of its system without overcoming or confusing another. Everything in existence is in motion within this scheme, behind which is the unfathomable, eternal Allah. The best state to be in is plunged in glorification (*tasbīh*) of the Creator, bewildered, in awe before the revolving circularity of existence, moving in harmony with it at all times.

$$\text{وَءَايَةٌ لَّهُمْ أَنَّا حَمَلْنَا ذُرِّيَّتَهُمْ فِي ٱلْفُلْكِ ٱلْمَشْحُونِ ﴿٤١﴾}$$

41. And a sign for them is that We bore their race in the laden ship.

The historical reference is to the people of the Prophet Noah. It could also refer to the human fetus which is carried in the womb. The Arabic word for 'ship' (*fulk*) is almost identical except for two vowel changes, to the word for 'orbit' (*falak*) in the previous verse in which the Qur'an says that the planets literally 'swim' in their orbit though we have translated the words as 'Each follows its orbital course'. Ships also float but in an environment of water rather than atmosphere. The natural links in creational events are reflected in the language chosen to express them faithfully.

The Arabic word *mashhūn*, translated here as 'laden', means 'filled up' or 'charged', suggesting that everything is charged and moving forward toward its mission of perpetuating the Ever-Continuing (*al-Bāqī*). This is the meaning of having offspring (*dhurrīyyah*), it is the perpetuation of a divine event. When one is with one's wife or husband it is a divine worship. One should always begin the act of being intimately together with the Name of Allah, the Beneficent, the Merciful (*Bismillah al-Rahman al-Rahīm*). Thus the song of oneness (*wahdah*) is made physical and perpetuated. If this song is present in the inward, it will manifest in the outward as well, in our children.

$$\text{وَخَلَقْنَا لَهُم مِّن مِّثْلِهِۦ مَا يَرْكَبُونَ ﴿٤٢﴾}$$

42. And We have created for them the like of it upon which they ride.

Everything in existence is in orbit around or 'riding' upon something. The purpose of such verses is to jostle man's intellect so that he may reflect upon this incredible unity in diversity, in order that he may wake up to the high station of perpetual awe and glorification, and be in total awareness. Outwardly he moves about by riding in cars, trains and airplanes, on and over the planet, while inwardly riding the stars of Allah's Attributes into the inner cosmos.

$$\text{وَإِن نَّشَأْ نُغْرِقْهُمْ فَلَا صَرِيخَ لَهُمْ وَلَا هُمْ يُنقَذُونَ ﴿٤٣﴾}$$

43. And if We will, We could drown them, and then there would be no help for them, nor would they be rescued.

If the balance which governs this existence is disturbed enough they will all be drowned by Allah's decree. His will is manifest in the laws which govern everything visible and invisible: if people transgress those laws, they will be overcome, recycled and returned to the Source. The same is true inwardly. We can flounder in the oceans of our ego-self (the lower *nafs*) by not following the outward laws according to the proper conduct. Outer travelling on the sea has its courtesy — one must make sure that the boat is sea-worthy. The journey toward inner purification and awareness requires protection and fortification; otherwise one will drown in storms of doubt, despair and illusion.

But a time comes when the balance cannot be restored except by a cataclysmic event. When the prophet Noah came to his people charged with conveying the message of Truth, he told them that they must change course, otherwise it would be too late. He warned them that their actions would result in a dangerous reaction. Afterwards he turned to Allah and said; 'I have pleaded with them day and night, but they take no heed and are obstinate.' The answer to him was that if he could not rescue his people, then he should save his own life and those of who he was in charge. The wave of injustices that had been generated had reached its peak, and was now going to break over his people.

When one is in the boat of the Book of Reality, the Qur'an, navigated by the practice (*Sunnah*) of the Prophet Muhammad, the Messenger and the Message, one is assured safe passage.

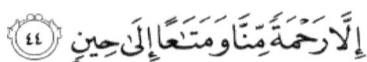

$$\text{إِلَّا رَحْمَةً مِّنَّا وَمَتَٰعًا إِلَىٰ حِينٍ} \quad \text{(٤٤)}$$

44. Except by mercy from Us, and as a comfort for a time.

Nothing will save anyone except the mercy of Allah. Translated as 'comfort', *Matā'* means the provisions one must take on a journey, imply that it is enough for a certain period of time only. The word also means 'baggage', because one only puts into one's baggage what is necessary for a particular journey. The verse says that if it were not for Allah's direct mercy and provision for this journey of life, all would have been drowned in the sea of ignorance. In reality, this time of comfort is but an instant.

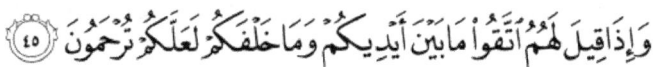

$$\text{وَإِذَا قِيلَ لَهُمُ ٱتَّقُوا مَا بَيْنَ أَيْدِيكُمْ وَمَا خَلْفَكُمْ لَعَلَّكُمْ تُرْحَمُونَ} \quad \text{(٤٥)}$$

45. And when it is said to them: Safeguard yourselves with fearful awareness against what is before you and what is behind you, so that you may receive mercy.

This is a warning to be cautiously aware of the actions one carries out, of what one forges with one's own hands, and of what the intentions are behind those actions, for every being in the present is the past personified. What lies before one is superimposed upon the past so as to become one's future. Thus one must be keenly aware of one's motives in any action, for this is what will bring about one's salvation or doom, and we are each busy manufacturing it in every instant. Our bird of evil or good omen, our cause of affliction or salvation, is within us, written by our intentions on the tablet of our actions.

One must be continually aware of this in order to experience inner contentment and understand the mercy of Allah directly in this life, because 'Allah has written mercy upon Himself' (6: 12). When one is constantly aware of what one is presenting and what one has already presented, then, through the recognition of cause and effect in the self, one begins to understand the laws of existence.

وَمَا تَأْتِيهِم مِّنْ ءَايَةٍ مِّنْ ءَايَتِ رَبِّهِمْ إِلَّا كَانُوا۟ عَنْهَا مُعْرِضِينَ ﴿٤٦﴾

46. And there does not come to them a sign from the signs of their Lord but that they turn aside from it.

This is as much the situation of the people of Antioch as that of the people to whom the Prophet Muhammad came and that of most times, including our own. Every sign that comes to us, pointing to the path of true existence, is rejected. We do not allow the message to get through and transform us. This verse is related to verse 11: 'You can only warn those who already follow the remembrance.' No matter what signs they receive from their Lord they turn away, because the only reality they want to face is that in which they have invested for so long, what they have built up for themselves in their private imagination (*wahm*).

وَإِذَا قِيلَ لَهُمْ أَنفِقُوا۟ مِمَّا رَزَقَكُمُ ٱللَّهُ قَالَ ٱلَّذِينَ كَفَرُوا۟ لِلَّذِينَ ءَامَنُوٓا۟ أَنُطْعِمُ مَن لَّوْ يَشَآءُ ٱللَّهُ أَطْعَمَهُ إِنْ أَنتُمْ إِلَّا فِى ضَلَٰلٍ مُّبِينٍ ﴿٤٧﴾

47. And when it is said to them: Spend out of what Allah has given you, those who reject and deny Reality say to those who accept and believe: Shall we feed one whom, if Allah willed, He could feed? You are in nothing but clear error!

The Qur'an continuously enjoins generosity and giving. Never does it say: Take!' or 'Acquire!' There is no reference anywhere in the Qur'an to going out in the world to make money or accumulate wealth, or anything even resembling this. The Qur'an is against accumulation. The Book of Reality, the way towards Reality, hinges on abandonment, not on the multiplication of desires and attachments. One must spend from that with which one has been endowed, so that it may spread. The principal concern is with sharing and caring, and the meaning of giving lies in giving what one loves and wants to keep. By spending one connects with Allah's all-encompassing Attributes of Mercy and Generosity.

Provision (*rizq*) implies numerous types of nourishment, be it the higher provision of inner knowledge or the lower provision of food and wealth. The highest provision of all is what comes to one directly upon truly abandoning oneself and being left without any will or expectations, remembering that one is born with nothing and leaves the world with nothing. The highest provision is the provision of true abandonment, true Islam, submission without a barrier, with no separation. This is knowledge of the Lord.

'Give out', does not only mean giving in charity. It also means being a conduit for Allah's mercy, emptying in order to be constantly replenished. Those who deny and cover up Reality (*kāfirūn*) seek to fix themselves to their possessions because they are living in separation: they see themselves separate from Allah. They see themselves as distant from their Lord because everything is perceived only in duality, so they say: 'Why does Allah not do it Himself?' Missing the point of existence, they fail to see how Allah acts in His creation, through His creatures. We are not separate from Reality, and Reality has neither beginning nor end. Allah is closer to us than our jugular vein. Only our bodies have a beginning and an end, but we falsely identify with our physical bodies through ignorance. This is the definition of denial and covering up, this is *kufr*.

Those who deny are at such a loss that it is almost

impossible to get through to them with the message of unity (*tawhīd*). They look merely on outward aspects of everything, failing to reflect upon subtle inner workings. Allah has decreed the creational laws, and those who follow His laws are connected to Oneness, while those who do not are at a loss and therefore suffer affliction though outwardly they may possess great material wealth.

وَيَقُولُونَ مَتَىٰ هَٰذَا ٱلْوَعْدُ إِن كُنتُمْ صَٰدِقِينَ ﴿٤٨﴾

48. And they say: When will this promise come to pass, if you are truthful?

Those who deny and cover up Reality are fooled by the illusion of time. Unable to recognize that the static perception of time is Allah's gift to man to enable him to experience non-time, they are in such a state of loss that they do not even remember that, at the end of the whole journey, man ends up under six feet of dust anyhow. Such people do not realize that man's life hangs by a thin wisp of breath.

مَا يَنظُرُونَ إِلَّا صَيْحَةً وَٰحِدَةً تَأْخُذُهُمْ وَهُمْ يَخِصِّمُونَ ﴿٤٩﴾

49. They await but a single shout, which will overtake them while they are disputing.

All this business of time is nonsense! Allah tells us that the question of time is relative and misleading. People will not see the point unless they experience the shout, the one, sudden, shuddering impact. This implies a complete break in the system. The one shout (*sayhah wāhidah*) breaks the system of life and time as experienced.

The one sudden shout is the first call which signifies the end of creation from the individual point of view. The second call, which is mentioned in a later verse, is the 'calling-forth', beckoning us to come forward and relive our actions and intentions. At this point we experience whatever we had invested in the short span of earthly existence. If we have yielded ourselves to the stream of mercy, we experience it, if we have invested in promoting the gross and material self, we shall be at a complete loss in this new life.

فَلَا يَسْتَطِيعُونَ تَوْصِيَةً وَلَا إِلَىٰ أَهْلِهِمْ يَرْجِعُونَ ﴿٥٠﴾

50. Then they will not be able to make a bequest, nor will they return to their families.

The arrangements they had made in their lives, their multiple plots and schemes are instantly cut off. It is too late for any return. No longer can they leave messages for people to carry out orders. They will be stopped in their tracks, absolutely helpless.

'Nor will they return to their families': not being able to return to their families means being unable to return to what is familiar. Their world has ended, there is no further possibility for action, and they cannot beseech anyone now for anything.

In Arabic death is referred to as *wafāh* from the verbal root (*wafā'*), which also means to be loyal. By dying one is loyal to the creational reality. A time will come when the soul separates from the body. The soul (*rūh*) returns to its source, to Allah, and our bodies return to the dust of which they are composed. In this way, creation is always faithful to its origin.

وَنُفِخَ فِي ٱلصُّورِ فَإِذَا هُم مِّنَ ٱلْأَجْدَاثِ إِلَىٰ رَبِّهِمْ يَنسِلُونَ ﴿٥١﴾

51. The trumpet will be blown, and then from their graves they will come forth to their Lord!

This is the second call, the call of Resurrection, the call to accountability. The first event is the private death or the end of one's own world. The soul remains in an interspace (*barzakh*) until the next phase, when the whole cosmos ceases to be and those energies which were inactive, the souls (*arwāh*), are suddenly activated and brought forth.

The signal is symbolized by a sharp trumpet-blast or 'horn' (*sūr*), because suddenly everything is cast up out of its place into clear view. Nothing can remain hidden in one's breast or in the grave. The sound of the beginning of the Resurrection announces the unification of the Seen and the Unseen. Separation between the secret and the evident no longer exists, for there is no longer any possibility of duality, of being separate from Allah in the experience of space-time. Only the absolute light of Truth shines out.

قَالُوا۟ يَٰوَيْلَنَا مَنۢ بَعَثَنَا مِن مَّرْقَدِنَا ۜ هَٰذَا مَا وَعَدَ ٱلرَّحْمَٰنُ وَصَدَقَ ٱلْمُرْسَلُونَ ۞

52. They will say: Woe to us! Who has raised us up from our resting-place? This is what the Beneficent promised, and the messengers told the truth!

The resting-place (*marqad*) can relate to the state of repose and tranquility which follows death. When this slumber-like state is violently interrupted by the trumpet, the sleepers are awakened to a supra-consciousness, a post-mortem condition. The *marqad* also relates to the slumber of ignorance of those who denied the message of Reality throughout their physical existence.

The response to their question of 'Who raised us from our sleep?' is: 'The Beneficent, as He promised and verified through His messengers'. This response can be seen in three ways. Some commentators say it is the response of angels, others that it is the response of those who were in true faith and submission; yet others say it is the response of truth emitted from the sleepers themselves who had covered up the Reality which they knew deep within themselves.

إِن كَانَتْ إِلَّا صَيْحَةً وَٰحِدَةً فَإِذَا هُمْ جَمِيعٌ لَّدَيْنَا مُحْضَرُونَ ۞

53. It is but a single shout, and then they shall all be brought before Us.

The first shout heralds the end of this life, the second one announces the universal entry into the interspace between death and the Resurrection, and the third reference is to being brought before the Divine Presence. Each time just one single burst of sound is referred to, for it is only one call, one action, one instant when all are immediately present before the One-and-Only Reality, which was there all the while. Now they see nothing other than One Essence. The event is described in three distinct parts, like the reverberations of an echo, yet as far as Allah is concerned the entire affair is the instantaneous divine Command: 'Be! And it is.' The decree is accomplished in no time but experienced by creation in stages.

Time has been created by Allah for our sake in order to evolve through its experience. We have been graced by this experience of time, so that those of us in self-abandonment can float in glorification (*tasbīḥ*), in the rising current, while those still attached to the stones of the self sink despite the current and drown.

Every spirit (*rūḥ*) will be present, for they have all come from one effulgent burst. Now that there is no longer any possibility of experiencing separation, all things are compacted again into that dense singularity that preceded the Big Bang.

فَٱلۡيَوۡمَ لَا تُظۡلَمُ نَفۡسٌ شَيۡـًٔا وَلَا تُجۡزَوۡنَ إِلَّا مَا كُنتُمۡ تَعۡمَلُونَ ﴿٥٤﴾

54. This day no soul shall be wronged in the least, and you shall not be rewarded but for what you did.

The word used here for 'day' is *yawm*, which also means 'time', 'period' or 'era'. In this context it refers to that next state, where the experience of duality is no longer possible, for in the non-space-time dimension there is only essence.

'And you will not be rewarded except for what you did.' Having loaded the scales with our intentions and actions in the previous life, we shall then see the result (*jazā*). We shall have earned our own reward and punishment. In the next phase, our intentions will manifest themselves fully and openly. Then, no person can cause injustice to anyone else, including himself, for the realm of action has ceased and all darkness and ignorance have been dispelled.

$$ \text{إِنَّ أَصْحَٰبَ ٱلْجَنَّةِ ٱلْيَوْمَ فِى شُغُلٍ فَٰكِهُونَ} \quad \textcircled{\scriptsize ٥٥} $$

55. Surely the companions of the Garden on that day will be happily occupied.

In the physical realm of existence they were also happily occupied, conscious of, and attending to, that affair of the final purification. The state of the Garden is attained when the remaining tarnish upon the heart is cleansed and purified.

$$ \text{هُمْ وَأَزْوَٰجُهُمْ فِى ظِلَٰلٍ عَلَى ٱلْأَرَآئِكِ مُتَّكِـُٔونَ} \quad \textcircled{\scriptsize ٥٦} $$

56. They and their partners will be in shade, reclining on raised couches.

Their souls are at peace for they have been paired with what neutralizes them and brings them rest. A pair (*zawj*) brings about oneness through union with its opposite.

'In shade, reclining on raised couches': affliction arising from duality is replaced by complete neutrality and utter tranquility. They are now in the shade (*zill*) of Reality, refreshed in the coolness of Oneness, the final refuge.

To those who first heard the Qur'an such verses were particularly meaningful, because the physical environment of the Arabs, where the earliest flowering of Islam took place, was the hot, arid desert, Cool shade was therefore considered to be conducive to bliss, relief and contentment.

$$ \text{لَهُمْ فِيهَا فَٰكِهَةٌ وَلَهُم مَّا يَدَّعُونَ} \quad \textcircled{\scriptsize ٥٧} $$

57. They shall have fruits therein, and whatever they desire.

In this state of freedom and bliss whatever they ask for is theirs. Whatever desire may arise is met with the object of the desire. This means that neither desire nor the agitation of possession remains.

$$\text{سَلَـٰمٌ قَوْلًا مِّن رَّبٍّ رَّحِيمٍ} \quad (٥٨)$$

58. Peace! A word from a Merciful Lord.

Peace (*salām*), greetings and acknowledgement from the Oneness of a Merciful Lord, is all that they experience. That acknowledgement is from the station of Lordship, as distinct from the Essence without Attributes.

$$\text{وَٱمْتَـٰزُوا۟ ٱلْيَوْمَ أَيُّهَا ٱلْمُجْرِمُونَ} \quad (٥٩)$$

59. And withdraw today, O wrongdoers!

By their denial and insistence upon their illusion (*wahm*) by continually dwelling within their self-built edifice in the material realm, by their not questioning its transiency and obvious impermanence, they wronged themselves. The more the senses are gratified and trained, the more they demand. The more we satisfy desires, the greater they become. Their analogy is fire: the more it is fed the hotter it rages, until it burns out of control. The opposite is the cool water of peace (*salām*), and this is the real meaning and purpose of Islam.

$$\text{۞ أَلَمْ أَعْهَدْ إِلَيْكُمْ يَـٰبَنِىٓ ءَادَمَ أَن لَّا تَعْبُدُوا۟ ٱلشَّيْطَـٰنَ ۖ إِنَّهُۥ لَكُمْ عَدُوٌّ مُّبِينٌ} \quad (٦٠)$$

60. Did I not charge you, O children of Adam, not to worship the Shaytan? Surely he is your open enemy!

Again the voice of Truth reassures by asking, 'Did I not give you My covenant? Did I not bind you to a contract, O children of Adam, not to follow that destructive energy that beckons you to what is fantasy and unreal? He is your open enemy from within! 'This state of energy referred to as the *Shaytān* in the

Qur'an and translated, but improperly understood, as 'Satan' in English, will constantly arise, The affliction of the *Shaytān* tests the resiliency of one's state, to see whether one's nature is ready for that inner bliss or not. Allah's creation is perfect, and Allah does not put anything in the wrong place. He does not bring one into that Divine Presence unless one is truly ready for it by inner awakening and distance from the whims of *Shaytān*.

We have the choice of falling into the slippery, enticing path of seeming ease or abandoning the project to the hands of the Beneficent, trusting that whatever comes is for the best, confident that one's inner and outer knowledge will be unified.

وَأَنِ اعْبُدُونِي هَذَا صِرَطٌ مُّسْتَقِيمٌ ﴿٦١﴾

61. And that you should worship Me. This is the straight path.

This is the direct route, the straight line, the shortest distance between two points, between what appears to be 'us' and Allah. This is the path of submission, the path of true abandonment. Derived from the Arabic verb *'abada*, used in this verse as 'worship', is the word *mu'abbad*, which means smooth or serviceable when applied to a road. When one is in worship (*'ibdah*, from the same root), in true adoration, there is no further resistance and the path to Allah is smooth and easy. Then the path does not appear as a line though the two dots are joined. We only see the line if we step sideways, but if the path is in line with our eyesight, the line no longer appears to be linear. Only a single dot appears, the dot of the letter *'ba'* of *bismillāh* (in the Name of Allah), because we have been truthful by the Name, and the Name is the indicator, the arrow pointing to the one dense singularity.

وَلَقَدْ أَضَلَّ مِنكُمْ جِبِلًّا كَثِيرًا أَفَلَمْ تَكُونُوا۟ تَعْقِلُونَ ﴿٦٢﴾

62. And certainly he led astray a great multitude of you. Were you not able to understand?

A great many nations and peoples have been, are, and will continue to be, at a loss. Does man not see, consider and learn from history and the experiences of his own life? The mercy of Allah is such that though a tree produces many seeds the majority do not germinate. Most people are like this, without the germination of the intellect (*'aql*), unharnessed and unable to think or reflect upon what is happening to them or to reflect on the signs that come to them from the outer or inner horizon.

هَٰذِهِۦ جَهَنَّمُ ٱلَّتِى كُنتُمْ تُوعَدُونَ ﴿٦٣﴾

63. This is the Hell you were promised [if you followed him].

ٱصْلَوْهَا ٱلْيَوْمَ بِمَا كُنتُمْ تَكْفُرُونَ ﴿٦٤﴾

64. Burn in it this day because you disbelieved.

The Arabic word for 'Hell' is *jahannam*, which means 'a bottomless pit', where there is not a moment's peace, a chasm (*hāwiya*) in which its inhabitants remain in a never-ending fall, like a parachutist in free fall, only the earth never appears and the parachute never opens.

This is the state of the next creation, a bottomless pit in which nothing ever settles. Man is programmed to seek stability in everything, in relationships, situations and knowledge. Essentially he is seeking permanency and reliability. The state of hell has neither, for it is absolute turmoil and incessant agitation. This is the endless Fire promised to man for denying Truth and for denying himself the light of knowledge, preventing natural awakening and enlightenment.

ٱلۡيَوۡمَ نَخۡتِمُ عَلَىٰٓ أَفۡوَٰهِهِمۡ وَتُكَلِّمُنَآ أَيۡدِيهِمۡ وَتَشۡهَدُ أَرۡجُلُهُم بِمَا كَانُوا۟ يَكۡسِبُونَ

٦٥

65. On this day We shall seal their mouths, and their hands will speak to Us, and their feet will testify as to what they have earned.

The tongues are silenced but the limbs bear witness to what they have earned. Whatever results from one's actions will be internalized in one's soul. Our being internalizes not only outward, physical actions but inward mental states as well.

From the healing sciences we know that if we take one cell from a part of the body, the hand for instance, we can tell the entire physiological story of the human being, From one cell of the hand, or even from the fingernail, it is possible to tell whether, for example, there is an imbalance or deficiency in one's overall condition and thus whether one is suffering from any diseases. Furthermore, the genetic fingerprint of each cell tells the entire story of the integrated system of the body, a kind of biological holograph.

Because every cell in the body tells the entire story of the individual it bears witness to one's overall state. The limbs — one's hands and feet — will therefore testify to the intention of the individual, why he was where he was and why he did what he did. One's actions are judged according to one's intentions. After death all physical power is lost. What was recorded in the cells of the physical body also made its impression on the spiritual body which now, in the zone of non-time and non-space, fully resonates with the reality of what it acquired. There is not even the mediation of verbal speech, which is subject to lies and therefore belongs in the zone of duality (time and space). Only the stark reality of what the self has earned is now recognized and experienced.

وَلَوْ نَشَآءُ لَطَمَسْنَا عَلَىٰٓ أَعْيُنِهِمْ فَٱسْتَبَقُوا۟ٱلصِّرَٰطَ فَأَنَّىٰ يُبْصِرُونَ ﴿٦٦﴾

66. And if We wished, We could certainly put out their eyes, then they would run about groping for the way, but how could they see?

If reality had been otherwise there would not have been either physical sight or insight. Use of the visible eye is the first means of apprehending sensible objects. From the sensible comes the intuitive, insightful faculty. The outer provides a means to serve the inner.

وَلَوْ نَشَآءُ لَمَسَخْنَٰهُمْ عَلَىٰ مَكَانَتِهِمْ فَمَا ٱسْتَطَٰعُوا۟ مُضِيًّا وَلَا يَرْجِعُونَ ﴿٦٧﴾

67. And if We wished, We could surely transform them in their place. Then they would not be able to advance or turn back.

This verse refers to the continued mercy and power of Allah. If He had wished He could transform human beings on the spot to reveal their true natures. However, He allows them to advance or regress.

Man contains within himself all the creational possibilities, both high and low. Man is a microcosm. Within him are all the characteristics that form the entire hierarchy of all living entities. When man does not conduct himself well and live up to the full potential of humankind, he falls into a lower state of animalistic tendencies in the creational hierarchy, for there is no such thing as stasis. He is either evolving or regressing.

Animals have been represented pictorially in several cultures of the world at some time or other, in the pyramids of Egypt, among the Zoroastrians, the Buddhists in China, in India and elsewhere. The sage or man of knowledge is often depicted riding on a chariot drawn by a dog and a pig, symbolizing his mastery over the lower tendencies of the self.

وَمَن نُّعَمِّرْهُ نُنَكِّسْهُ فِى الْخَلْقِ أَفَلَا يَعْقِلُونَ ﴿٦٨﴾

68. And whomever We cause to live long, We reduce him to an abject state in creation. Do they not use their intellect?

The Arabic word *'ammara*, translated here as 'cause to live long' also means 'to build, erect, construct, raise', *Nakkasa*, translated as 'reduce' also means 'to turn around, lower, withdraw and relapse'. The implication is simply 'what goes up must come down'. This alludes to the universal law of the cyclical nature of every individual entity and every creational system.

'Do they use their intellect? (*afalā ya'qilūn*)'. Do people reflect a little and are they thus able to see that with every upward construction there is also a downward construction, that every growth inherently contains its opposite process of decay? Using the faculty of intellect, it is not difficult to see that the realm of physicality and duality must have an opposite realm of non-physicality and non-duality, that is, a realm after the death of the physical body.

وَمَا عَلَّمْنَاهُ الشِّعْرَ وَمَا يَنبَغِى لَهُ ۚ إِنْ هُوَ إِلَّا ذِكْرٌ وَقُرْءَانٌ مُّبِينٌ ﴿٦٩﴾

69. And We have not taught him poetry, nor is it fitting for him. It is but a reminder and a clear recitation.

Though this verse is about the Prophet Muhammad and the Qur'an, it is also about us as well, about those who occasionally receive glimpses of the glorious gift of self-awakening in which one apprehends higher realities. The Arabic word for 'poetry' is *shi'r*, from the verbal root (*sha'ara*) which also means 'to feel'. The verse states that the Prophet Muhammad's message is not poetic, emotional or sentimental. Poetry is not fitting for prophets. A prophet (*nabi*) is a man who gives other men news (*naba'*) from the timeless zone of another consciousness. The Prophet is an agent of remembrance (*dhikr*) of a knowledge that is already within us and he removes the veil of ignorance and darkness. The word translated as 'recitation' is Qur'an, that which is read or recited as a reminder. The Qur'an is a reminder which polishes the interior of the heart so that what is inherent within it — one's own reality — is clearly reflected.

The Qur'an cannot be compared to even the highest poetry. It is direct revelation (*wahy*) from the Divine Source, through the Angel Gabriel, to the trustworthy (*amīn*) Messenger of Allah.

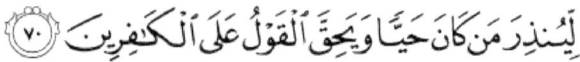

$$\text{لِيُنذِرَ مَن كَانَ حَيًّا وَيَحِقَّ ٱلْقَوْلُ عَلَى ٱلْكَٰفِرِينَ ﴿٧٠﴾}$$

70. To warn whomever is alive, and to prove the word true against those who conceal Reality.

The implication here is that what one normally considers to be life is not necessarily full or 'alive'. The automatic, physical activity of the body is not the state or condition of being truly alive, it is merely the lowest level of life. One may be in a breathing, heart-beating physical form and yet be inwardly dead. There is a story of a spiritual master who was walking with a seeker and the master began pointing to people, one after the other and saying, 'There's nobody at home, there's nobody at home.' Finally, the bewildered seeker asked him what he meant, and the master replied: 'They are inwardly vacant, inwardly dead.' The warning can only come to those who are alive to what is going on around them and within themselves, to those who can hear and who are in good heart.

The Qur'an says of itself: 'Certainly it is a bounteous clear recitation in a book kept hidden. None may touch it except those who are purified' (56: 77-79). 'Those who are purified' does not only mean those in a state of ritual ablution (*wudū*), which is a precondition for physically touching the Qur'an. That condition is necessary, but, deeper than that, the verse refers to those who are focused on reality and are completely present and alive to what is going on at the moment. When one's mind is somewhere else, not fully concentrated on what is present, one gives life to an illusion of the imagination and is dead to the reality of what is really present; when the mind is constantly worrying about yesterday or tomorrow, one is not present but wrapped up in illusion. So where are we?

A person who follows his own idiosyncratic, biographical book rather than the 'Book', misreads the read-out of Reality which is open to him in every instance of pure, unadulterated presence. One can therefore only give the warning, the news, to those who have the spark of vibrant life (*hayāt*) in them. The meaning of Islam is 'submission'. If one is in a state of complete submission, then one is not afraid or anxiety-ridden but fully present, and consequently, fully alive.

This verse echoes verse 11, and in this reinforcing way the Qur'an constantly circles back on itself to illuminate its meaning further: 'You can only warn someone who follows the reminder and fears the All-Merciful in the Unseen.'

'And to prove the word true against those who conceal Reality': the word, the truth, will be proved against 'those who deny or conceal Reality'. The Qur'anic term of *kāfir*, refers to someone who has something in his heart but covers it up in some way. Covering up means adding some other godhead or focus of worship, whoever or whatever it may be, one's family, country, wealth and possessions or reputation, and not allowing the innermost to unify with one's outermost. *Kufr*, is denial of *tawhīd* (unity). The very actuality of *kufr* or covering over Reality implies the inherent presence of the unitary potential as the substratum of the human project. The warning of the final doom is addressed to those who deny. They themselves will be denied, forever fettered by the chains of their denial because of the limitations which they sought to impose on Reality. Once the possibility of change is removed through death, the possibility for them to get out of that prison also vanishes.

أَوَلَمْ يَرَوْاْ أَنَّا خَلَقْنَا لَهُم مِّمَّا عَمِلَتْ أَيْدِينَآ أَنْعَـٰمًا فَهُمْ لَهَا مَـٰلِكُونَ ﴿٧١﴾

71. Do they not see that it is We Who have created for them — out of what Our hands have wrought — grazing livestock, which are under their dominion.

The word for grazing livestock *an'am* is related to the verb which means 'to live in comfort and ease' (*na'ama*) and the noun *ni'mah*, which means 'blessing or bounty'. *An'am* specifically refers to cattle, sheep, camels and goats. According to the traditions of early Islamic culture and Prophetic practice we are limited in the numbers of domestic and wild animals we can use and eat. The same is true of fish. If this were not the case, our stomachs would become the graveyards of all kinds of creatures.

Allah says in this verse that these animals were created from 'Our hand', 'Hand' here means 'from the action of creation'. Can man not perceive these animals, so useful to him and easily brought under his control as signs of Allah's mercy and wisdom? Reflection shows the Hand of Reality behind all the bounties which have been given to him for his use.

وَذَلَّلْنَـٰهَا لَهُمْ فَمِنْهَا رَكُوبُهُمْ وَمِنْهَا يَأْكُلُونَ ﴿٧٢﴾

72. And We have subjected these animals to them, so some of them they ride and some they eat,

As far as man is concerned, he is the master of the animal kingdom. Man has been exalted even as a creature of flesh, for he is the superior being, while animals are subject (*dhallala*) to his domination. All animals under his control must be used in specific ways, each within certain limitations that complement each other, enabling man to live with sufficient provision. Man is given his food, shelter, clothing and mobility so that he can then glorify the Creator of all creation, acknowledging in adoration that all comes from Him.

وَلَهُمۡ فِيهَا مَنَـٰفِعُ وَمَشَارِبُۖ أَفَلَا يَشۡكُرُونَ ﴿٧٣﴾

73. And from them they have [other] benefits [besides], and yet they get [milk] to drink. Will they not then be grateful?

Man benefits in many ways from these bounteous creatures. Everything from the hide of a cow to its milk can be beneficially utilized. These verses clearly imply that the entire creation is subservient to man who is the ultimate creation, provided he raises himself to fulfill the potential within him to be the vicegerent of Allah on earth. He has the option of demeaning himself to the condition of a timid, sub-human creature or raising himself to a station above angelic existence. The best way to attain to the higher state of man's potential is by recognizing Allah's manifestation in all things and by not forgetting the gratitude we owe to Allah for what He has provided, whether in difficulty or ease.

وَٱتَّخَذُوا۟ مِن دُونِ ٱللَّهِ ءَالِهَةً لَّعَلَّهُمۡ يُنصَرُونَ ﴿٧٤﴾

74. And they have taken [other] gods besides Allah [hoping] that they might be helped.

These gods (*ālihah*) refer to any object, tangible or intangible, which one adores unduly, anything one is besotted with or connected with in a more than normal manner. We may adore sleep, but we do not think about it all the time. This verse refers to any situation or object which one exalts, giving it a higher, frequently superstitious, value.

People who have taken '[other] gods besides Allah' are at a loss, and they include the majority of humankind. This is something we are prone to doing. Those at a loss place undue trust in illusory entities in the hope that they will afford them the ultimate solution and happiness.

When standing up for the ritual prayer we recite *Allāhu*

Akbar, which means 'Allah is the greatest!' This confirms that
we have searched everywhere to find the greatest thing in this
existence and have found only its eternal Creator to be worthy
of worshipful acknowledgement. *Allāhu Akbar* means that
Allah is greater than anything we can conceive.

$$\text{لَا يَسْتَطِيعُونَ نَصْرَهُمْ وَهُمْ لَهُمْ جُنْدٌ مُحْضَرُونَ ﴿٧٥﴾}$$

75. They have not the power to help them; but they will be brought forth as an army.

All these other things which we think are going to save us or
help us — family, wealth, position, country or whatever — are
just temporary reliefs. We have come from the womb and our
bodies are on their way to the tomb. In between, we must wake
up and recognize the oneness that encompasses this journey. It
is the way and plan of Allah, and if one thinks one is safe from
the plan of Allah, then one is in a state of ever greater loss:
'They plan and Allah plans, and Allah is the best of planners'
(3: 54).

These deities we consider so important will never be able
to save us, even if they had at their disposal extraordinary
powers, soldiers or energies. Any power we might ascribe to
them still falls within the limited domain of this world, which
is under the dominion of the source of all power. They cannot
save us in this world, so how can they possibly save us in the
next world?

$$\text{فَلَا يَحْزُنكَ قَوْلُهُمْ إِنَّا نَعْلَمُ مَا يُسِرُّونَ وَمَا يُعْلِنُونَ ﴿٧٦﴾}$$

76. So let not their speech grieve you [O Muhammad]. Surely, We know what they hide and what they openly manifest.

Do not be afflicted when they mock you. Do not care about
falsehood. During the early years of his prophethood there
were no more than a dozen, or at most twenty, people with the

Prophet in Mecca. At the time, he was already over forty years old, but it was neither the number of followers that counted nor the number of his years.

People tend to cling to their false ways and habits in order to hide their own fears and ignorance, frequently attacking others as a way of doing so just as the people referred to in verse 30 attack the threat to their illusions and attachments with the weapon of mockery. But as Allah says here, 'We know the reality, or the instigation, behind what they say, so do not be saddened by the denial of those who deny the truth.'

Allah knows that these people hide within themselves the agony of their disconnectedness and that what they say is only an attempt to affirm that state of incongruence with their original nature (*fitrah*). They are separated from their inherent nature, but observe the perfection of Allah's underlying ways; they are unified with their own rejection and denial. One of the great Muslim philosophers *Haydar 'Amulī* said: 'All of existence occurs according to unity (*tawhīd*). It is the source of the path of Islam and the means for attaining both the Garden and the Fire.' The one who denies Reality advertises his own destiny.

'There is no controversy or dispute about Islam,' says the tradition. One is either in Islam or out of it. The real Muslim does not enter into controversy. He only sings his inner song, and if it is heard, it is because those who hear it have the right listening apparatus to tune into that waveband. But if they do not have the apparatus, that spark of real life (*hayāt*) within them, they cannot hear him. People who are on the true path of calling others to Allah (*da'wah*) are never disappointed. They say: 'It is Allah's concern, not ours.' Such a person has abandoned himself to his creational song.

أَوَلَمْ يَرَ الْإِنسَـٰنُ أَنَّا خَلَقْنَـٰهُ مِن نُّطْفَةٍ فَإِذَا هُوَ خَصِيمٌ مُّبِينٌ ﴿٧٧﴾

77. Does man not see that We have created him from a sperm-drop? Yet behold! he becomes an open adversary.

The verbal root of *insān*, the word used here for man, means 'to be companionable, familiar, intimate'. Man naturally wants familiarity and intimacy, which means that he seeks personal and social fulfillment and the interconnectedness between himself and all other beings, between himself and all existence. He therefore instinctively shrinks from what he does not know, from the unfamiliar. His primal urge to unify expresses itself in the wish to unify his intentions with his actions.

Allah asks, 'Does man not recognize his own creation from the sperm, the lowest of the low, yet within this physical vehicle is the genetic program, the chemical alphabet in which the message of creation is encoded?' The prophetic message of the Qur'an explained the biological cause of man's origin long before modern science did, and at a time when what passes now for the scientific, rational world was filled with superstition. The word for sperm, *nutfah*, means a living cell.

But instead of seeing by the wondrous physical nature of his own creation that Allah has created him by His command, man inclines to argument and quarrel. Enmity (*khusūmah*) is a natural phenomenon of the lower self of man. This condition of enmity comes naturally to every person because no one likes to be confused, uncertain or dependent upon somebody else. Thus he bites the hand that feeds him. He wants independence, because inwardly there is an echo of Allah's Attribute of Sublime Perfection, His Self-Sufficiency. Allah is the Giver, the Lord of all, not one's father or mother.

Traditional Arab culture recognized this independent aspect of man, which is a positive characteristic when transformed, for it produces strength, courage and resourcefulness. In order to nurture it properly, urban dwellers would take their young boys away from their mothers at an early age and place them in the temporary care of a desert-dwelling family. Healthier for the child was an environment where the negative social influences of town life were eliminated, and the smothering affection of the mother was also minimized. The child would continue to go back and forth from his home to the desert until about the age of seven. In this way, the natural instinct for independence was nurtured in a gradual, positive way.

$$ وَضَرَبَ لَنَا مَثَلًا وَنَسِىَ خَلْقَهُۥۖ قَالَ مَن يُحْىِ ٱلْعِظَٰمَ وَهِىَ رَمِيمٌ ﴿٧٨﴾ $$

78. And he coins a similitude for Us and forgets his own [origin and] creation. He says: Who will give life to these bones after they have rotted away?

The argumentative man asks, 'Who is going to recreate the bones when they are dispersed and decayed?' 'He has forgotten his own creation!' Allah declares. Is the re-creation of man after death more miraculous or difficult than his creation in the first place? All the elements of the planet were contained within the fertilized egg from which he developed. Though science has now described the process of formation in the womb, it is still baffling how this creature called man came about, from a fertilized egg! Whoever had the power to form him originally can certainly re-create him in another way.

$$ قُلْ يُحْيِيهَا ٱلَّذِىٓ أَنشَأَهَآ أَوَّلَ مَرَّةٍۖ وَهُوَ بِكُلِّ خَلْقٍ عَلِيمٌ ﴿٧٩﴾ $$

79. Say: He will give life to them Who brought them into existence in the first place, and He is the Knower of every creation.

The baby in the womb is in such a benign state, leading such a comfortable existence, that it does not want to come out. Soon, however, his continued growth causes him to emerge with a cry, because his support system has changed. Suddenly, the mouth which had been useless for nine months in the womb becomes necessary. The ears which have never heard anything before but the constant beat of the heart in remembrance of Allah are called upon to distinguish an endless variety of sounds. The eyes open and must become accustomed to light. So this verse says: 'The One Supreme Knower Who created in the first place can give life again in any form He chooses!'

He Who brought it together and constructed it in the first place has knowledge (*'ilm*) of the entire creation, both outwardly and inwardly. He knows what is outside us and what we are hiding deep within us. He knows all the uncertainty and confusion of those who deny. He has the blueprint for every creational entity. He is *al-'Alim*. For every creational pattern He knows all the programming and can reconstruct it from scratch, so why do we persist in our assumption that the life of this world is only eating, sleeping and death?

$$\text{ٱلَّذِى جَعَلَ لَكُم مِّنَ ٱلشَّجَرِ ٱلۡأَخۡضَرِ نَارًا فَإِذَآ أَنتُم مِّنۡهُ تُوقِدُونَ ﴿٨٠﴾}$$

80. He Who has produced for you fire from out of the green tree, and behold! you kindle with it [your own fires].

Once again Allah calls man to look at another creational cycle with which he interfaces and from which he obtains direct benefit. The green tree is transformed so that it can be kindled by fire. By this example we are being taught to look at opposites. Out of water comes fire: the moist green tree, the major constituent of which is water, dries and enters a different phase, from which come the heat and dryness of fire. Water and fire are thus linked together, even though they are polarities. Their opposite qualities normally cause one to dominate the other. Either water puts out fire or fire boils water until it disappears as vapor. The nature of creation is so sublime that even things so diametrically opposed, through a transformative phase, can come together in a process beneficial to man.

This verse is an analogy for the spiritual purification of the self; that is, the green wood that is transformed by death into a medium suitable for the burning flame of Divine Love. It can also be an analogy for those who deny the reality of the Fire in the next life. Cannot He Who created the green tree, and by its death made it kindling wood suitable for fire, do the same for man?

$$ أَوَلَيْسَ ٱلَّذِى خَلَقَ ٱلسَّمَـٰوَٰتِ وَٱلْأَرْضَ بِقَـٰدِرٍ عَلَىٰٓ أَن يَخْلُقَ مِثْلَهُم بَلَىٰ وَهُوَ ٱلْخَلَّـٰقُ ٱلْعَلِيمُ ۝ ٨١ $$

81. Is not He Who created the heavens and the earth able to create the like of them? Yes, indeed! And He is the Creator [of all], the Knower!

From the proof of the self s reality, Allah moves on to the horizons of the heavens and the earth, as He says; 'We shall show them Our Signs on the horizons and in themselves until it is clear to them that it is the Truth' (41: 53). It is a rhetorical question: He Who created the earth and the celestial universe, can He not create the same all over again? That energy, that situation which came about due to His command, can it not be repeated just as easily as before? The deeply resounding voice of Reality answers: 'Yes, indeed, for He is the Creator, the Knower!'

$$ إِنَّمَآ أَمْرُهُۥٓ إِذَآ أَرَادَ شَيْـًٔا أَن يَقُولَ لَهُۥ كُن فَيَكُونُ ۝ ٨٢ $$

82. His command, When He intends anything, is that He says to it: Be! And it is.

His command, the command for creation from the Essence of Reality is 'Be!' By simply having intention, the entire creation issues from His command. Divine intention itself is the beginning and the end. From it alone stems the whole creation. If, within the ocean, the wave energies are such that a new wave is to be formed, everything moves spontaneously towards bringing that about, and a new wave swells up. The necessary elements are intention or will, which is the basis of change and movement, and the inherent ability to accomplish the action.

$$\text{فَسُبْحَٰنَ ٱلَّذِى بِيَدِهِۦ مَلَكُوتُ كُلِّ شَىْءٍ وَإِلَيْهِ تُرْجَعُونَ ﴿٨٣﴾}$$

83. So glory be to Him in Whose Hand is the dominion over all things, and to Him you will return.

How can we not glorify Him? What other course is there but to be in a state of glorification of Him in Whose hands, in Whose dominion lie the control and total possession of everything! From Him we have come and to Him we return. We have no real duty but to be consciously in glorification. The Arabic word for glorification, *tasbīḥ*, is also the name given to the string of beads used by the faithful to help invoke remembrance of Allah. These beads are only a means of aiding concentration for the repetition of whatever formulae or Divine Names used. The point of regular remembrance is that it eventually becomes natural to do it all the time. Our glorification must be constant, because wherever we look, whether we like it or not, everything is coming from Allah. Not only what we like is from Allah but also what we do not like. If something undesirable presents itself before us, it is only because we have ignorantly transgressed and gone into territories we were not supposed to enter, and thus we experience the rebound or rectification of that deviance. Every creational system produces an equal and opposite reaction. We always deserve what we get. The love of Allah strikes us to remind us when we have moved off the balanced path. It is Allah's love warning us not to remain in harm's way but to return to safety.

There is nothing to do but be in a state of continuous glorification (*tasbīḥ*), to swim through life in submission. The verbal root of the word *tasbīḥ* is *sabaḥa*, which means 'to swim'. Islam is conscious, intelligent, wakeful, diligent submission, not apathetic resignation. Submit intelligently and then see the signs. They all indicate only love for us, therefore we cannot reciprocate with anything other than glorification and gratitude. If in any state other than this, we are at a loss, and there is nothing to blame but our own ignorance or denial.

So glory be to Him! Bewilderment is our destiny. By seeing this bewildering, breathtaking panorama of creation, we are lost in wonder. We can only glorify and be positively lost in this unfathomable unfolding, both visible and invisible. We are completely bewildered in the ocean of this amazing situation, kept alive in the hands of Him Who has perfect control over all things. It is cosmos not chaos, in perfect balance at all times. We shall all return to Him Who created us. From Him we have come, by His grace we are sustained and to Him we return. This is the good news. We are not separate from Him. We are by Allah, from Allah, and to Allah: there is only Allah, the One-and-Only Reality. Access to Him is through total abandonment of every veil, concept, worldly relationship or security which one considers important and real, including one's own self.

CHAPTER 36
Surat Yā Sīn: Summary

Sūrat Yā Sīn — The Safe Abode of Protection for the Day of Resurrection
We find that the Qur'an is the supreme manual for living in this world, thereby preparing us for the next world, a world beyond time and measure. He who has been blind in this world, who has not been able to discern the laws that govern existence in this realm, will never be able to gain insight into the subtler realms, which, though less tangible, are instrumental in governing this world.

Sūrat Yā Sīn gives us vivid teaching of the ways of Allah. It contains a full description of unity (*tawhīd*), the nature of Reality, the laws that govern existence and the extent of man's freedom as a being which can encompass the Seen and the Unseen Worlds.

The chapter begins by addressing the Prophet, symbolically using letters from which language is constructed making human communication possible. Language differentiates human consciousness from creative consciousness and letters serve as the building blocks of language, in the same way that atoms serve as the building material of the molecular substructure of physical existence. Letters and atoms both form interconnected patterns adhering to particular laws of 'spelling' and 'grammar', by which all creation has unfolded, in the sense of meaning and in form. The literal components parallel and symbolize the chemical alphabet present and active in genetic material that gives matter a meaningful form.

The formulation of man's destiny is made clear to us by

the meaning of bad or good omens, as the messenger who was sent to Antioch said: 'Your doom is brought down upon you by your own actions!' Wittingly or unwittingly, man dictates his own destiny. We are the microcosm and we are the doers. Everyone of us is the center of his or her own universe, for everything in the world of experience connects to us. Our world is what we deserve it to be. Not everyone is able to hear this, not everyone can get the message or, having received it, dive into its depths. The barriers against full perception are of one's own construction and are as thick, as strong and as deep as one's expectations, desires, fears and anxieties. In other words, they are in inverse proportion to the purity of our submission to the Lord of Reality.

We have also seen in this chapter that the qualification for a person to impart true knowledge is that he should expect no reward from anyone. He must also have already come to know the basic, underlying factors of reality in this existence. He is enlightened and self-realized.

As we progress, we find that fear (*khashyah*) is actually the result of uncertainty, of not knowing where the boundaries of behavior lie. By the practice of Islam, fear can be transformed into incremental degrees of faith (*īmān*), until certainty (*yaqīn*) about the essential nature of Reality emerges. From this certainty develops a cautious or fearful awareness (*taqwā*), for once one has tasted certainty one would never wish to step outside its bounds. The person who has followed the path of the prophetic message and has fully awakened to the meaning of Reality completely believes and trusts that all is well. Soon he begins to witness and experience that, in fact, all is well. Subjectively he may continue to have likes and dislikes, but the truth of every matter is that whatever has happened has happened, therefore it was correct, for it faithfully followed the laws governing the occurrence of that event. If we examine the steps leading up to any event, its outcome would be comprehensible, whether we like it or not.

There are no exceptions to these laws. When the first Muslims were in battle, the arrows found the Prophet Muhammad just as they found others. The arrow struck his teeth and broke them, making his mouth bleed. The arrows did not suddenly stop in mid-air just because he was a great prophet of Allah. Natural laws in this existence are such that the physical prevails over the subtle. One's basic needs must first be met before one can turn to one's higher, subtler needs. Everything has its proper natural flow (*ādāb*). We move from the gross to the subtle; first comes the health of the body, then the mind, and then the intellect and the spirit.

In *Sūrat Yā Sīn* we also find a reinforcement of the view that we dictate our own destiny. The voice of Reality says: 'And We do not send down unseen powers or angels from the heavens nor do We ever do so.' This implies that by our own intentions and actions we bring about final results. If our actions are incorrect, in the sense that they do not follow the flow of intended natural laws, we are bound to bring doom down upon ourselves.

Nature is effulgent and expansive. We all echo the Big Bang. The whole cosmos is exploding in expansion, so if we do not grow within ourselves in inner joy we shall end up sick, for we shall not have followed the creational decree. If we do not explode our illusion, we shall not dissolve into the magnificent, unending, expansive bliss.

'A fountain from which the slaves of Allah drink, making it gush forth abundantly' (76: 6): this is what true nourishment for the heart is all about. If we do not echo the cosmic expansion within our own being, we shall end up suppressed and self-oppressed, and we will implode and collapse upon ourselves in a perverted way. A vivid example was the destruction of the people in the city of the Prophet Lot. They were homosexuals, decadent, abandoned to wanton lust and perversion. Since nature's way is expansive, that is to say, the natural order is that of increase, the constricted and dissipated energy of this people created a situation around them that ultimately caused their destruction. Their chosen mode of behavior was contrary to nature, and that energy itself caused the natural catastrophe that brought about their end. Nature only affirmed their injustice to themselves with an outer parallel of their inner disconnection. This is not superstition, it is unity (*tawhīd*). We are not separate from the cosmos; our actions affect the entire cosmos as we interact with it, and the secret of all our actions resides in our intentions.

In the Qur'an we find that good actions done with pure intentions, without expectation of reward, result in an unquantifiable reward. Wrong actions, on the other hand, result in a requital of equivalent value. The river of movement which we experience in time flows in a certain direction. Anything dropped into that stream flows in harmony with that direction and becomes magnified. Speaking in the direction of the wind, for example, the voice is magnified. Speaking against the wind simply obliterates any sound. The wind of destiny carries Allah's manifold blessings. Anything moving with this breeze is at one with the decree and will grow and endure.

The laws which govern existence will sooner or later overwhelm us if we transgress them either inadvertently or ignorantly, whether aware or unconcerned; our task is to know the laws, where to draw the line and how to get back on to the straight path. It is said that the straight path (*al – sirāt al-mustaqīm*) is sharper than the blade of a Damascus sword. The sharpness implied here is in awareness, constant, perpetual, self-effulgent awareness for its own sake, not an awareness of any particular created being. To begin with, one may be aware of one thing or another but awareness of some things is, in fact, distraction (*ghaflah*), for one may then miss other things. If, however, one is spontaneously aware of the self, one is open and available. In this state, the knowledge one needs in any circumstance will automatically be manifest.

As creatures of action in this world, we seek to unify

inwardly in order to have access to knowledge that is useful, knowledge that springs from spontaneous awareness, knowledge that helps us in the arena of action, so that we move more and more towards liberation. Although we are born free, without asking for life, and we die without knowing beforehand where, when, or in what circumstances, yet, in between these two major events, we find ourselves shackled by chains of expectation and desire. The more we shackle ourselves inwardly the more we exhibit an outward arrogance to defend the flimsy edifice we have built. Yet the whole object of life's exercise is to abandon oneself and dissolve into the one-and-only sublime consciousness. When one lets go of lower consciousness, movement and passage toward higher consciousness instantaneously take place.

In the same way that we move on in age we can also move on in meaning, moving from one state of meaning to higher ones, in an ever-ascending, self-perpetuating continuum. If sensitive enough, we shall find meaning in every breath and in every occurrence that takes place in front of us. But, generally, we are insensitive. If we do not seize it as it passes, it may have gone forever and we have missed it. With every split second, with every breath, Allah is bestowing meaning upon us in order to show the total ecological balance in the oneness of this existence.

Ecology does not end at the border of our property, the national border of a country, or the border of the body's skin. Ecology is multidimensional and universal. We each affect the entire global ecology and the world, in turn, affects us. There is no separation. Separation exists only in the individualized biological sense, since these particular cells are encased in the sheath of this particular skin. The skin, however, is breathing and alive. It is being influenced by the surrounding atmosphere, just as what surrounds it is being influenced by the being that occupies it. Creation is a total, ecological transaction in which the creational system of boundaries is based upon the boundless reality. Limitation is only meaningful because of the limitless. The abundance of nature can only be enjoyed if we set limits to how we abuse it.

The way to unveil or unfold the meaning of this life in order to grasp the essence is like peeling an onion. The meaning of existence is encoded in our genes, but in order to read the genetic code we must look at successive layers of existence. Each layer is a world of its own. These worlds of states and stations are what we have given meaning and objective reality to. When we peel the first layer of the onion, there is another layer, then another layer, and then yet another until, when we arrive at the heart of the onion and unfold the last layer, there is only pure space. Space is also what existed outside the onion, and at the same time the onion is permeated by space, exactly as we are permeated by Reality. There exists only that one Reality.

Things only have the appearance of materiality because of the mind's faculty of the imagination (*khayāl*) which allows us to solidify objects. In reality, creation is essentially space, much more fluid, more dynamic. Of course, our everyday world of solid objects does exist. This existence, however, is only a secondary existence. It is only a shadow or hologram of its essence.

We contain within ourselves the meaning of non-existence and limitlessness as well as the meaning of existence and limitation. Normally we exhibit more limitation and dependency, which is what causes us such difficulty. This is the sickness of mankind in this realm. Our purpose for coming into this existence is to evolve out of it, by recognizing the One Reality. This existence is not an end in itself. All the prophets tried to impart to mankind that God is, has been, will be, and that as we come from the Divine Being, we contain within ourselves the potential to awaken to the meaning of Allah's limitless, unfathomable glory. If we address ourselves to the lower end of the scale of existence, we shall experience only the lower end of creation. If we address ourselves to the higher end, we shall see ourselves in relation to the unity from which we sprang and unify the outer with the inner consciously. We are the interspace (*barzakh*) between the high and the low, between this world of limitation and the limitless hereafter. By turning towards the high, the low is purified and transformed.

By turning towards the low, it is magnified and the high obscured: 'Those who do not witness falsehood and when they pass by what is vain they do so nobly' (25; 72).

Man is the only creature whose consciousness spans both dimensions. Confusion arises in this life out of the apparent paradox that while we are limited and coming closer to the grave with every breath, at the same time we want the eternal. In all our pursuits of wealth, love, knowledge or happiness we are seeking that quality of everlastingness because we echo the eternal within us.

The Qur'an says that Allah encompasses everything. This means that everything is absorbed in godliness. Because existence is based and balanced on opposites in existence, we cannot gain consciousness of the boundaries of transgression, and understand the all-pervading godliness, without the presence of evil and wrong action. Man brings about results in any particular situation according to his actions taken within the context of that situation. Man's actions provide the pegs which nail the entire affair together.

If we have no expectations and no desires, we are freer than a bird. Most people, however, usually react. Since we each have a certain set of wants, we each react according to the impinging forces and stimuli that come from outside and which, by interacting with our own particular profile, produce results. If there is no personal, individuated profile, as symbolized by the position of prostration (*sajdah*) in the ritual prayer, which when performed with pure and sincere concentration means the complete obliteration of the ego-self, one is on the path of freedom. This does not mean, of course, that we do not differentiate in the outward world between what is good and bad.

'And surely you will have a reward without end' (68: 3): if our hearts are throbbing and pure, and we genuinely take life on as a journey and an adventure in the path of Allah, all of it is a delight. We shall be surrounded by like-minded people who echo that outlook. But if we are self-centered and fearful, we shall attract people of the same resonance. Birds of a feather flock together; this is the law of nature, this is Allah's unchanging way (*sunnah*) in the creation, and we cannot escape it.

Freedom cannot exist in this life without constraints. Health cannot be understood without illness. Freedom in the abstract cannot exist. The meaning of the proverb, 'Trust is the bondage of free men' (*al-thiqah withāq al-ahrār*), is that outer courtesy and limitations ensure inner freedom and salvation.

If we seek freedom, we must find its roots which lie in its opposite, in enslavement. The laws of opposites constantly apply. We must trust that although we may not comprehend them now, we shall come to know these laws more and more. This is one aspect of *īmān* (trust, faith).

Allah manifests Himself in the laws which govern existence, since they are unifying laws which apply to all. If someone claims to be a gnostic (*'ārif*), or enlightened, we assume that he knows the laws that govern existence, but the laws governing existence are from beyond existence and greater than existence itself, otherwise existence could not be encapsulated in them. The real meaning of gnosis is total abandonment and submission. The gnostic, by his abandonment, comes to know what is necessary for him to know at the time he needs to know it. The gnostic's ego-self or *nafs* does not alter his capacity to receive guidance. He is abandoned. He has given up. Thus he is automatically and perfectly tuned.

In this chapter, the meaning of the Garden (*al-Jannah*) is made clear. It is that hidden, secret state where the heart can be tranquil as a result of pure abandonment. This does not mean physical abandonment, leaving one's family destitute or not caring about how one dresses or behaves. Even if one goes to a cave in the mountains one will find that the mind is still agitated. True abandonment comes about gradually, by standing up to responsibilities, by doing one's best and not being inwardly attached and by not yearning for the results of one's actions. All is done in the way of Allah (*fī sabīl Allāh*). From this perspective an action such as marriage is only useful in the passage of this wonderful journey of life if each person writes upon his or her heart that he or she will help their partner to be content and to realize inner freedom. It is almost a state of worship, as indeed every action should be. There is nothing wrong with agitation and passion per se. Without passion in this life, there would be no yearning. But one's passion should be for knowledge, for Allah, because the existence of all human beings is conditional upon the Independent One, Transfer love for the creature to love for the Creator.

True compat*ibi*lity comes about when a man and woman genuinely want to collaborate and serve each other, freely, for the sake of truth, knowledge and inner freedom. Inner freedom cannot be obtained without outward courtesy and respect. Unless we constrain ourselves outwardly, we cannot grow inwardly. Should one want inner freedom, one must expect outer limitation. False, outward freedom is capricious. It can only cause chaos, both outward and inward. Thus, as the seeker approaches knowledge of Allah his actions become more restricted. His wish is to act within the correct boundaries. His heart takes him to the goal, but to get the heart into the proper state requires being linked with what is harmonious.

Everything in creation is governed according to the laws of nature, and the name given to the Giver of the law is Allah. Access to Allah is by understanding and following His laws inwardly as well as outwardly. An outward orientation is not enough. The external pattern only provides indicators or information, not self-knowledge. A real spiritual teacher's job is to crack the shell of ignorance that envelops the seeker. He merely removes some of the rust that has been veiling the heart from the source of light within. The spiritual guide does not give anything; he only removes something: Allah said: 'The heavens and earth do not contain Me, but the heart of the believer (*mu'min*) contains Me.'

This, then, is the remedy we obtain from *Sūrat Yā Sīn*. Those who do not get the point of this life will eventually get it when they die. This is why this chapter is read when a Muslim dies, in the hope that his spirit (*rūh*) is sufficiently tuned to remember or resonate with its original reality, the remembrance of which is ingrained within it.

This short life is only a link in the chain of being. Before this life there was a mode of existence, and after this life there is another mode of existence. The nine-month period in the womb connected us to this realm; the sleep after death, expressed by the verse 'Who has raised us from our place of rest' (36: 52), connects us to the next. Does anyone clearly remember the experience of the womb? In the same way, we cannot remember the non-experiential state to which we are returning.

This inability to remember what came before or to know the reality of life after death leaves the person of reflection bewildered since every human being with intelligence questions what this experience of life and death is all about. 'Why am I unhappy? Why am I not self-fulfilled? Why am I not inwardly free?' Causing us agitation is part of Allah's mercy. It is Allah's will that we should come to know Him Who disturbs us and thereby brings us out of our physical and animalistic lethargy. Every problem we have is really a gift to us from Allah's love.

The man of Allah prays to his Lord, 'Please give me responsibilities so that I can progress and mature in life,' When problems are taken on outwardly with a positive attitude, spiritual movement occurs. This entire existence is but a single drama, and all beings are the actors in it. The way to transcend the drama is to stop acting out whatever role a person thinks is his and to take appropriate action and assume responsibility for Allah's sake (*fī sabīl Allāh*), without any personal motives. In this way one avoids adding layer upon layer of illusion. The best way to overcome illusions and assumptions and other similar veils is to confront situations in the way of Allah without expecting any reward. Events in life act as chisels to open up the layers of the self. Eventually, one finds that what there was at the center of it had been there all the time.

In reality we only have duties in this life, we have no rights. We only have obligations. We are squandering oxygen at an enormous rate. Every few years we each consume several tons of it. The question is, have we consumed it in order to burn out our expectations and desires and find our way to inner freedom? If we have not, then we have squandered the natural gift of creation. The same is true for the tons of food we consume. Are we nourishing ourselves in order to obtain strength to know the Divine Reality in every state and manifestation?

The removal of ignorance is a prerequisite for enlightenment. If this veil is not discarded in this life, it will be eliminated at the time of death. On the Day of Resurrection 'no self will be wronged' because action is no longer possible and we each shall be accountable for our own actions. Time and motion will be frozen, and the self will reflect what it has earned. At that moment, the soul will sing out what has been engraved on it through the person's actions and intentions while alive in the world. Nothing can be added and nothing can be subtracted. If one has echoed the pure song, in the next life this song will simply be heard forever in Allah's Garden. But if the soul is a marred disc, full of arrogance, ignorance and confusion, the song will reproduce this quality of use. The soul in the Hereafter sings the level of its attainment in the life of the world.

The key to purifying the heart from ignorance is spontaneous awareness of intention. That way one's intentions unify with one's actions. This represents the station of freedom through submission and presence. This is unity (*tawhīd*) and sincerity (*ikhlās*).

Be willing to die now, and you will live! Be willing to give up everything, and you will find that everything is already available. Behind all multiplicity there is only oneness. Each person contains the chromosomic imprint that has within it the laws governing the entire cosmos. This is the real 'I'. The Qur'an is within us, but one must plunge into and dissolve in it and discover that everything is resolved, not solved, for there really is no problem. There is no god but Allah! Know the essence of beingness and you will find only freedom. It is we who construct our cages, so only we can dismantle them completely and we do so by transferring our actions to the realm of free and pure undertaking, fearlessly and courageously.

When one fully understands one verse of the Qur'an, one has understood the whole Qur'an. All the analogies and metaphors (*amthāl*) in the Qur'an echo the Truth, so why not plunge into the Truth? We and what we have plunged into are not separate. *Sūrat Yā Sīn* stresses that those who have earned the Garden were engaged in a pure affair. They had no business other than being self-fulfilled. In the Qur'an, metaphors are used to describe the indescribable, for language operates in the realm of duality, of cause and effect, of content and container. Metaphors gracefully take one aboard the ark of meaning to the edge of reflection, where one must throw off all restraint and make the quantum leap into the shore-less sea.

Some of the repeatedly used metaphors of the ultimate Garden are mates, fruits, couches and shade. Everything in existence occurs in pairs. Unification can only take place where there is a pair, which is the symbolic reason for marriage. Shade is regarded as a very desirable aspect of nature, particularly in desert environments, for it offers respite from heat and a place of restful retreat. Whenever we encounter verses about reclining on couches or cushions, the meaning of such sitting can be inferred. The cushion has no value in itself, but sitting on a cushion or reclining on a couch in the shade means one is in a relaxed state. The body is forgotten to some extent, and one's consciousness has the opportunity of being less physically orientated, so that one can go into the realm of meaning. We neutralize the material and physical in order to reach the meaning within.

Whatever we desire is a figment of our imagination (*wahm*). Having spun our own web, we have invested our time and energy in that web: 'And surely the frailest of houses is the spider's web if they but knew!' (29: 41). If a sincere seeker were able to achieve everything he wanted in this existence, whatever it might be, he would eventually reach a point where he would not want anything, because everything he wanted would be already here. After true reflection he would come to the point of desirelessness. He would know that everything was available to him, that all the fruits he could possibly hunger for were already there, and that consequently he would desire no more. This is the meaning of the description of the contentment in the Garden of Paradise.

The message is very simple. Just be (*kun*), and the whole world will come to one (*fa yakūn*). Knowledge and contentment is within. Outwardly and inwardly there is only mercy and blessedness. Should one see other than perfect harmony and blessedness, it is one's own distorted view, one's own web which has separated one from its perception. The state of the higher Garden is peace, tranquility, bliss and eternal contentment, peace that has been promised from a Merciful Lord.

And Allah knows best!